Living in

the U.S.A.

ALISON RAYMOND LANIER

INTERCULTURAL PRESS INC.
70 West Hubbard Street
Chicago, Illinois 60610

Library of Congress Catalogue No. 72-2212
ISBN 0-933662-10-6

Printed in United States of America

Author's Note:

This book stems from conversations with countless people from all over the world. I am grateful for their thoughtful contribution to it.

This book was first published in 1973 by Charles Scribner's Sons. Since then it has been revised, up-dated, and republished in English paperback editions three times—this is the fourth updating and fifth edition. It has also been published in seven other countries and languages.

It has grown out of the experience of my own firm, Overseas Briefing Associates, which has worked for many years with U.S. and foreign personnel, helping them adjust to unfamiliar countries and conditions. Recently OBA became the international arm of Moran, Stahl and Boyer, a relocating consulting firm at 355 Lexington Avenue, New York. Our work continues there both with Americans going on assignments to other parts of the world and with foreign nationals coming to the United States.

SPECIAL NOTE TO READERS FROM CANADA, MEXICO, CENTRAL AND SOUTH AMERICA

To fellow Americans from other parts of the hemisphere—my apologies!

Throughout this book I have used the word "American" many times to mean "of the United States," with the full knowledge that the United States is only a *part* of the Americas. The trouble is that we have an unwieldly and difficult name to use! It is cumbersome to keep saying "North American," and in any case this includes Mexico and Canada too. It is impossible to say "United Statesian!" So please forgive my inaccurate and not necessarily inclusive use of the word "American." It is done through no lack of appreciation or awareness of all the many customs, cultures, and countries that are equally American.

Table of Contents

Part II

PRACTICAL POINTERS

Part III

FOR THOSE WHO STAY LONGER

"The point of change is to see from a deflected angle, with a different focus, what has been familiar and habitual."

—ALISTAIR REID

Part I

AMERICAN INTANGIBLES

a. that cannot be touched
or grasped, esp. that cannot
be grasped by the mind

AMERICAN INTANGIBLES

First Impressions

Jet airplanes circle the world. News is bounced off satellites so that we literally "see" each other more and more clearly in our homes and varied lands. Naturally such developments lead to increasing business among nations. With this comes the transfer of negotiators, salesmen, heads of companies, students—often accompanied by spouses and families.

Transfer to the United States is often a difficult transition. Things move fast, spaces are great, variations are confusing, Americans speak with many tongues. The position of children, teenagers, and old people in American social patterns is often unexpected by others. The daily mechanics of living are bewildering. Why must one have insurance? What about household help? What are the pitfalls in buying a car? What kinds of taxes must be paid? When? What customs and courtesies are different?

PACE

For many people the pace of life is what is most confusing, especially at the beginning. One's first impression is likely to be that everyone is in a rush—often under pressure. City people appear always to be hurrying to get where they are going, waiting impatiently to be served a meal, restlessly seeking attention in a store, elbowing others as they try to complete their errands. At first this may appear rude. Bus drivers will be abrupt, waiters will hurry you, people will push past you. You will miss smiles, brief conversations with strangers, small courtesies.

errand — short journey made to get sth. or to carry a message
do~, run~ for. e.g. I've no time to run~ for you

5

Don't take it personally. The pace is gentler outside the big cities, as it is in other countries as well.

Americans who live in cities assume that everyone is equally competitive and self-sufficient; they expect others to "push back" just as city people do in Tokyo or Paris, in Beirut or Sao Paulo. But the minute they discover you are a stranger, most Americans become quite kindly and will take great trouble to help you. Many of them first came to the city as strangers and they remember how frightening a new city can be. If you need assistance or want to ask a question, choose a nice-looking person and say:

"I am a stranger here. Can you help me?"

Most people will stop, smile at you, and help you find your way, or advise you in whatever is needed. *But you must let them know that you need help;* otherwise they will pass you unseeing and unheeding, wrapped in their own concerns. A few may not respond helpfully. If this happens, don't be discouraged; just ask someone else. Most Americans enjoy helping a stranger.

heed. vt. pay attention to; n. attention. pay ~ to, give ~ to
roll: an official list of names. **PEOPLE**
        call the ~

Who are these people who are swirling around you? Some 230 million of them now call America home, but in fact they have their origins in every part of the world. The names you see over shop doors tell you so, as do the varied types of faces you pass on the streets. A roll call of school children will include such names as Adams, Ali, Bykowski, Capparella, Fujita, Gonzales, Mukerji, Nusseibeh, and Wong. Mostly these diverse backgrounds have not mix been blended in the so-called American "melting pot." In fact the idea that America is a melting pot is largely a myth. What exists more often is a kind of side-by-side living in which ethnic groups retain many of their own customs and social traditions. They merge into the American stream only in certain aspects of life—in schools, sports, business, and science, to name a few—but keep to many of their own customs and patterns socially and at home. Many tensions now apparent in American life stem from the interplay of varied cultures. The plus side of this situation is the richness that comes with variety, the wide freedom of choice that exists in ideas and dress, in food and customs. The minus side is that unseen barriers do still exist for some people, most often in the worlds of business and housing—particularly at lower income levels. Nonetheless, everyone can find his own familiar world here—be it in spices or fruits, churches or national groups, newspapers or music.

INFORMALITY

Although American informality is well known, many interpret it as a lack of respect when they first encounter it, especially in the business world. The almost immediate use of first names, for example, jars on nerves long accustomed to deference or respect from men of lower rank.

Don't be surprised if Americans do not shake hands. They often just nod or smile instead. A casual "Hi" or "How are you doing?" or "Hello" often takes the place of a formal handshake, but it means the same thing. Nor will you find Americans circulating about a group in the office or at a party giving each one a personal farewell. Instead—again the different sense of timing and pace—they will just wave a cheery "good-by" or say something informal to the whole group such as "Well, see you tomorrow" or "So long everybody." Then they will disappear. No handshakes.

Often you will see men working at office desks in shirt-sleeves, sometimes without their ties. They may lean far back in their chairs and even put their feet on the radiator or desk while they talk on the telephone. This also is not meant to be rude. Once we get out of the tense, hurried city streets, we are a loose-jointed, informal, relaxed people.

Our pace is total—either totally hurried, intense, work-absorbed, and competitive (in play as well as work), or else totally at ease, relaxed, "laid back" and informal , our manner breezy. We tend to swing between these extremes. This is the pendulum you need to understand if you are to understand America and its people.

SIZE

It is difficult to really experience or "feel" the size of the United States even when you know the actual number of miles from coast to coast. To get the full impact, one should realize, for example, that it takes 48 hours (two long days and two long nights) to travel by train from Chicago to Los Angeles, rolling along hour after hour across wheat fields, mountains, and deserts. Chicago is a full overnight train trip from New York.

Another way to think about it is to compare distances in the United States with others more familiar to you. For example:

New York to Washington, D.C., is about the same as:
   London to Paris
   Nairobi to Mombasa
   Tokyo to Kyoto
New York to Los Angeles is farther than:
   Lisbon to Cairo
   Moscow to Montreal
   New Delhi to Rome
New York to Chicago is close in distance to that between:
   Manila and Hong Kong
   Berlin and London
   Buenos Aires and Asuncion

It is difficult for those people who come from smaller countries to realize what a factor this matter of sheer size is in the life of the United States. Not only is the country vast in extent, it also contains 230 million people. This affects every phase of life—not only creating a highly competitive internal market for goods—which gives rise to constant advertising—but also a far-flung and equally competitive political arena. Wide geographic differences make for profound differences in attitudes and values. A traditional New Englander, for example, is as different in point of view from a Texan as is a Portuguese from a Finn, or an Indonesian from a Korean. Marked differences in geography or weather and widely dispersed ethnic heritages naturally affect peoples' attitudes—but in the United States such differences occur within the same nation. An overseas visitor once remarked: "No wonder Americans talk so loud and move so fast; in a place that size you almost have to or you get lost in the shuffle."

Size always affects psychology, whether it be among individuals or nations.

TIME ZONES

Another way to comprehend the vastness of the continent's size is to be aware of the time changes that take place as one moves across it. There are four different time zones between the two coasts:

When it is 12:00 Noon Eastern Standard Time in New York, it is
11:00 A.M. Central Standard Time in Chicago,
10:00 A.M. Mountain Standard Time in Denver,
9:00 A.M. Pacific Standard Time in San Francisco.

Canada, being wider from east to west, adds two more time zones, Atlantic Standard Time for New Brunswick, Nova Scotia, and Quebec; Yukon Standard Time for its extreme western provinces.

Alaska (the forty-ninth state of the United States, but not adjoining) extends even farther west than Canada and adds an additional two time zones: Alaska Standard Time and Nome Standard Time. Hawaii, (the fiftieth state) is a group of islands in the Pacific Ocean, about 2400 miles west of the United States mainland. Since it is immediately south of Alaska, it falls in the same time zone.

Time zones circle the world, an hour apart from each other. There are 24 around the earth, based on the "meridians" (or longitude lines) which start at Zero Meridian, which passes through Greenwich, England. The American continent is so wide that it encompasses *one third* of all these time zones.

The world's Date Line is halfway around the world from Zero Meridian, that is, 12 hours away from Greenwich, on the 180th Meridian. Luckily for all of us, the line runs for the most part through the open Pacific—the most convenient spot it could be! East of this imaginary line, the calendar is a day earlier than points west of it. People coming to the United States from Asia will therefore add a day to their lives—until they go home again!

CLIMATE

Naturally, with such distances, the climate in the continental United States also covers great extremes. From New England and New York through Chicago and most of the Midwest and Northwest, temperatures vary from sub-zero in winter to the high 90's or over in summer (Fahrenheit).

The South, Southwest, and California have warmer weather, though even these sections have occasional frosts and periods of moderate cold. Speaking generally, you should be alert to the fact that summers are likely to range from 70°F to 100°F (21°C to 35°C) and in many areas can be quite humid. However, air conditioning is so widespread that you can expect most buildings—even private homes—to be kept at relatively comfortable temperatures.

Alaskan temperatures are, of course, extremely cold most of the year while Hawaii enjoys a very moderate climate. Temperatures are normally in the seventies (Fahrenheit).

Chapter 2

Customs Vary with Cultures

Many American customs will catch you offguard; the same thing happens to us when we visit another country. People living in varied cultures handle many small daily things differently. What a dull world it would be if this were not true!

Some differences are minor, and one soon becomes accustomed to them. At first, for example, Asian women may be startled at having their hair washed and dressed by men; visitors may be amazed to see men wearing wigs; people may find the transitory quality of much of American life odd—the fact, for example, that one can rent art by the week or the entire furnishings of an apartment, from sofa and beds to the last spoon, on less than eight hours' notice."Packaged" living is part of today's American scene, part of its mobility and pace.

At the same time—and perhaps even *because* of this sense of impermanence—houses interest Americans greatly. They spend much time thinking and reading and talking about the design of houses, their decorations, how to improve them. Many weekend hours are passed in "do-it-yourself" projects around the house. People love to inspect each other's houses. Since they would thoroughly enjoy visiting and examining a house in another country, they assume that you will probably have the same desire. Don't be surprised, therefore, if you are shown the entire house from top to bottom, including bathrooms and closets! Americans think they are doing you a favor. Don't make the mistake of refusing; the whole house may have been tidied up especially for you!

DOING YOUR OWN THING

Because our people have come from so many nationalities, there is a far wider range of what is "acceptable" than in some countries

11

where the inhabitants have grown up with a common heritage. As a result, no one needs to feel awkward or uncomfortable in following his own customs. Although Americans are noticeably informal, if you prefer somewhat greater formality, feel free to act in your own way. This will be acceptable to those around you. As the young say, each person can "do his own thing" and be respected here to a very large extent.

However, it may help to have a little guidance in understanding the normal pattern of customs in the United States The subject is, of course, too broad to cover fully, but the following are a few common situations you may encounter.

PERSONAL QUESTIONS

Conversational questions may seem to you both too personal and too numerous—especially when you first arrive.

"Where do you work?" "How many children do you have?" "Do you play golf?. What is your score?" "Have you taken your vacation yet?" are not personal questions by American standards. They are a search for common ground on which to build a relationship or base a conversation. Understand that such questions are meant to be friendly; the questioner is interested in you and is not prying or being impertinent, or at least not deliberately so.

This is the way in which we ourselves become acquainted with one another. Since many of us move around the country so often and meet so many people in the course of a year, we tend to "telescope" these exploratory courtesies. We meet, and by rapid questioning we establish what we feel to be an easy understanding, for we know that in this fluid society we may soon loose touch with this person in the normal ebb and flow of life.

In less mobile countries people operate from a different basis. They erect defenses of a social nature to protect their privacy and their position; they hold off any moves toward intimacy until there has been adequate time to assess the newcomer and weight him in the balance. Only then do they feel comfortable in discussing anything as personal as their children, or where they live, or what they do at work. The difference is more of timing than of intent. Americans move faster, living like a movie that is run at double speed, because tomorrow they may be tranferred across the country or you may be back across the sea. "If we flow apart again, we will at least have had today," say the Americans.

To those coming from countries where introductory amenities are normally handled more slowly, ever a longer period of time, the American way can seem like an abrupt barrage of questioning, almost frightening in its personal intensity yet even here there are subjects which are avoided, being considered too personal and therefore impolite. These include questions about a person's: age; financial affairs; cost of clothes or personal belongings; religion; and love (or sex) life.

If you are asked these or any other quesitons which seem to you to be too personal, you need not answer them. You can simply smile or say pleasantly that you "do not know" or "In my country that would be a funny question," or turn the questions gently aside by some comment such as "Isn't it interesting to see how different nationalities begin a conversation?" or some similar deterrent. If you do that, follow it quickly with another topic, or make some comment of your own on variations in customs, or lead the conversation off in some other direction. The American will not be offended, but he will get the point.

INSTRUCTIONS

The whole matter of names is a "culture shock" to many people. Americans have little feeling for "rank," especially social rank. Most do not themselves enjoy being treated with special deference for age or position; it makes them uncomfortable. Many Americans find even the terms "Mr.," "Mrs.," or "Miss" stiff and formal. You hear people well beyond middle age say—even to quite young people—"Just call me Sally (or Henry or Don)." Being on first name terms is taken as a sign of acceptance and friendliness.

However, this need not bother you. If you are not comfortable in following someone's immediate request to "Call me Andrew," it is quite all right. Just smile and say "after a while perhaps, but thank you anyway" (meaning, for feeling that friendly!).

Quite normally, introductions are made right from the start with first names: "Mary Smith, this is John Jones." This then leaves the option open to you; you can call the lady "Mary" or you can call her "Miss Smith"—whichever you prefer. Sometimes both of you use last names for a few minutes, then one or the other (or both) lapse into first names. The host has given you the choice. If you don't want to use first names so quickly, just don't. Nobody will mind.

As "women's liberation" becomes a strong movement in the U.S., women are referred to more and more frequently with the indeterminate title: Ms. (pronounced "MIZZ"). This is considered the female equivalent of "Mr." (Men are not identified by whether they are married or not, so why should women be?) Most women still accept (and some prefer) the traditional titles, but don't be surprised if you meet women who do not.

You may notice that when Americans speak together they almost never use each other's names or titles in conversation. We have no equivalent to "Alors, Mademoiselle. . ." If you are accustomed to hearing such forms of address interspersed though a conversation, their lack may feel cold or impersonal at first. Feel perfectly free to drop in your own "Madame," "Senor," "Herr Doktor," or the actual name if you want to do so. It will sound "interesting," different and a bit flattering to the American! But do not be offended if we do not do it too.

TITLES

Waves of people who have come to settle in the United States have discarded the whole concept of "high and low estate." Status titles are associated with class distinctions—Lord Apley, Count Bernard, the Marchioness of Something. Since class differences are minimized in this country, we do not have family titles, although we comply if visitors carry them. What we do use instead, if a person is distinguished, are *occupational* titles. These are considered to be different, denoting a recognition that has been *earned,* not merely inherited. Occupations which most frequently carry titles include: diplomats, members of the Senate (or certain other top government posts), judges of the courts, military officers, medical doctors, ranking professors, priests, rabbis, and some Protestant clergy.

Examples would be: Ambassador Jones, Senator Smith, Governor Rockefeller, Judge Harley, General Clark, Dr. Brown (medical). Dr. Green (Ph.D.), Father White, Rabbi Cohen, Dr. (or Bishop) Gray.

Generally speaking, men in all other occupations are addressed as "Mister," women as "Ms." If in doubt as to the manner of address, never hesitate to ask. If you are embarrassed about asking, yet want to be respectful, you can always use "Sir" or "Ma'am." The people you address will probably realize your dilemma and help you by telling you the proper term.

But unless you are distinguished you will find all formalities in address are quickly lost. You will not hear Herr Studienrat or Directore or Senora for long because a friendly, informal relationship is more important to Americans than is either rank or status. We can still respect a person deeply even if we call him Charlie or Pedro. To us, respect and informality are not related.

DEFERENCE

There are other customs in addition to a disregard of titles that visitors accustomed to considerable attention and service at home may find insulting at first. Some people may feel that insufficient deference has been paid them in relation to their position when they are treated like everyone else here. Since the United States is a "do-it-yourself" country, we generally carry or own bags, take our laundry to the laundromat, stand in line at the grocery store, or shine our own shoes, whoever we may be—lawyer, professor, bank

president, or corporate executive. Service in the States is purely a
matter of cold cash; it has nothing to do with deference, respect,
position, race, nationality, or personality. Whoever can afford the
extremely high cost of service in this country and wants to buy it,
may. But there is absolutely no social stigma in doing one's own
daily chores, no matter how menial. In fact, many Americans who
could afford household help or a driver or a gardener do not employ
them. They prefer family privacy, independence, freedom from
responsiblity, all of which are at least partially lost when one has
help in one's home. Others would rather use their money for travel,
sport, or in some other way instead of paying high American wages
for domestic help.

Domestic help, on the other hand *is* available (especially cleaning
women) for those willing to pay. You may have to search hard for
someone satisfactory, however. Ask your neighbors or colleagues
how to find them when you get your own home.

PROTOCOL

Similarly, those coming from countries where rank is clearly
recognized feel the lack of protocol. We do not bow more deeply, or
a greater number of times, to some people than others to show
respect; we rarely seat an honored guest in a particular position in
the living room or in a car. The few formalities you may observe are
that the "honored guest" will normally sit to the right of the host or
hostess at a dinner party and will probably be shown through a door
or into an elevator first. However, if this causes any delay or blocks
the passageway, the nearest person (rather than the most honored)
may often go through first without implying any disrespect at all.

In Japan the back seat is the honored place in a car. If we have any
feeling for this at all, it likely that the front seat, next to the driver,
is considered the best in a private car, partly because the driver is
likely to be the host and partly because the front window offers the
best view.

BLUNT SPEECH

Because we Americans come from varied backgrounds, many of us lack full social graces and have remarkably small vocabularies. Don't think we are being rude if we tend to speak in monosyllables or answer with a mere "O.K.," "Sure," or "Nope," or greet you with "Hi." Our brevity is not a personal insult, though to those accustomed to gracious phrases we are (and will seem) blunt. How much more courteous it is to use the Japanese phrase "Osore irimashita"—"I am overpowered with admiration"—in a shop, for example, than just to say "Too expensive" and turn away. Both make it clear that since the price is too high the speaker is not going to buy, but the Japanese way is undoubtedly more gracious!

You may also be surprised and perhaps offended at the swearing and references to sex you hear from people whom you would not expect to talk that way. In contemporary America swear words and words related to sex have become commonplace. Let's hope it is a passing phase!

WE ARE EASILY EMBARRASSED

Americans are sometimes blunt from embarrassment too. They often find it awkward to respond gracefully if people compliment them or thank them at any length. They are likely to brush aside such courtesies and "turn people off" out of embarrassment; not as experienced or poised as one would expect, they simply do not know what to say! Their intent is not to be rude; in fact they really like your courtesy but cannot express a graceful response. Except for Christmastime, there is not a great deal of gift-giving in the United States, so you will find Americans may be embarrassed as they accept gifts, especially if, being unprepared, they have nothing to give you in return. We are, on the whole, a warm but unpolished people!

SILENCE

Many Americans find silence uncomfortable. They will babble on to fill any quietness if it extends for more than a moment. Students often study with their radios blaring; housewives leave television on for the "companionship" of sound even though they may be working in some other room. If you are silent for long periods, they will do their best to "draw you out" or will ask if you feel all right or if there is anything they can do to help you. One aspect of silence can be confusing however: if Americans disagree with what you are saying, many of them will remain quiet. This may not indicate agreement; often it only means that they consider it impolite to argue further.

PRIVACY

Often perplexing to those newly arrived from other lands is our lack of desire for privacy. We are not a nation of hedges and walls, of gates and inner courts. Our lawns run into one another without fences; we leave our office doors open while we work; we run in and out of each other's houses without telephoning first, often without even ringing the doorbell.

This is a big country. Its inhabitants have never lived in walled cities or had to protect themselves from warring princes in neighboring states. During our first centuries, America was so sparsely populated that neighbors were something to be longed for—they were not fenced out. A new face or new arrival was a cause for rejoicing. In the covered-wagon days when this nation was first being developed, people lived cooperatively or not at all. They turned their wagons inward and came together in the circle of firelight for safety. They protected one another, they shared their sweat and labor jointly as together they cut down forests, laid railroads, roofed barns, or husked fields of corn. They deeply depended on each other in all phases of life.

Out of these early days has come a heritage of openness rather than privacy. It shows itself in many little ways. You will feel it as you visit in our houses—rooms without doors or with half walls, no walls, or glass walls. We feel the opposite when we travel; we are surprised to find doors constantly shut throughout homes and offices. Part of the answer may lie in central heating. The thing to remember is this: lack of concern for privacy is a difference of custom to be understood but not to be fretted over. If colleagues wander into your office without knocking, or if people enter your office without knocking, or if people forget to close your door when they leave the room, don't be upset. Help them to learn that you would like it to be otherwise, or else adjust yourself to new ways. But in either case, be patient with the practice. It goes a good deal deeper into our roots than even most of us realize. Most Americans actively *dislike* the feeling of being enclosed in a room. They prefer an open doorway; unconsciously they miss a sense of space, a feeling of "breathing room," the sounds and flow of everyday life. They feel, as they say, "boxed in" when they find themselves in a tightly shut room. "Don't Fence Me In" could be our national song!

DISTANCE AND BODILY CONTACT

Did you know that all human beings have a "comfort zone" regulating the distance they stand from someone when they talk? This distance varies in interesting ways among people of different cultures.

Greeks, others of the Eastern Mediterranean, and many of those from South America normally stand quite close together when they talk, often moving their faces even closer as they warm up in a conversation. North Americans find this awkward and often back away a few inches. Studies have found that they tend to feel most comfortable at about 21 inches apart. In much of Asia and Africa, there is even more space between two people in conversation. This greater space subtly lends an air of dignity and respect, an amplitude of time. This matter of space is nearly always unconscious, but it is interesting to observe.

This difference applies also to the closeness with which people sit together, the extent to which they lean over one another in conversation, how they move as they argue or make an emphatic point. In the United States, for example, people try to keep their bodies apart even in a crowded elevator; in Paris they take it as it comes!

Although North Americans have a relatively wide "comfort zone" for talking, they communicate a great deal with their hands—not only with gestures but also with touch. They put a sympathetic hand on a person's shoulder to demonstrate warmth of feeling or an arm around him in sympathy; they nudge a man in the ribs to emphasize a funny story; they pat an arm in reassurance or stroke a child's head in affection; they readily take someone's arm to help him across a street or direct him along an unfamiliar route. To many people—especially those from Asia or the Moslem countries—such bodily contact is unwelcome, especially if inadvertently done with the left hand. (The left hand carries no special significance in the U.S. Many Americans are simply left handed and use that hand more.)

In all such matters, however, if it disturbs you, a slight hestitation on your part will usually be felt and heeded.

In much of the world, handholding and kissing in public have become commonplace. Certainly it is true in the States. One merely ignores what one sees and passes on.

MOTION

Americans are a restless people. Most travel whenever they get the chance. Until gas shortages and prices curtailed them, they drove hundreds of miles at the drop of a hat. No longer able to do this, many are chafing; some are changing to gas-efficient cars or motor bikes; others are crowding onto overtaxed trains, buses and planes, despite soaring prices. In increasing numbers, others take to their feet or bicycles with packs on their back, heading for the mountains, seashore or national parks. Still others are beginning to explore their own localities, joining the millions of tourists who flock to the United States from abroad. The dollar value has changed so markedly that secretaries, construction workers, and blue collar workers from many parts of the world are now able to travel as well as the rich—and they do. Over two million foreign travelers (a record high) visited New York alone in the past year, according to the New York Visitors Bureau. The number of tourists is expected to continue its rapid upward climb in the years ahead.

Don't be surprised if you are crowded and jostled by throngs of travelers, Americans as well as those from all over the world.

Chapter 3

Some Dominant American Attitudes

CRITICIZING AUTHORITY

In much of the world, authority is not challenged either out of respect or out of fear, sometimes, too, because a hierarchy of rank has been fixed for so long that people have been trained for generations never to challenge it.

In such countries children are not expected to question their teachers in school, and brilliant young scholars or inventive industrial geniuses are hampered in technical research because they hesitate to disagree with their "superiors." Clever researchers may be considered too young or have "any right" to present findings that contradict knowledge and wisdom of their elders.

The American is trained from childhood to question, analyze, search. "Go look it up for yourself" a child will be told. School tasks are designed to stimulate the use of a wide range of materials. An assignment to "Write a paper on the world's supply of sugar (or the gold standard, or Henry VIII, or Peruvian art)" will send even a young child in search of completely unfamiliar ideas. Even in the primary grades, children are taught to use libraries, and to search for new ideas. By the time they are 14, 15, and 16, many young scholars are making original and valuable contributions in all fields of science from astrophysics to oceanography. Industry is so aware of this untapped resource that each year, through national competions, it offers tremendous awards among teen-agers in order to seek out (and later employ) the brilliant, inquiring minds which they find scattered across the country.

As seen by members of other nations, this emphasis on questioning and searching is bad for young people's "manners." Foreigners often feel great "lack of respect" in our youth. It is true that many do become cocky and rude and pressing. Foreign visitors are often startled and frequently annoyed to find junior staff members "daring" to challenge older executives or argue points with them; they do not always like it when these young men make detailed but often revolutionary suggestions. One's own blueprints, reports of analyses may be scrutinized in detail—perhaps even challenged—by a young person. This is not to be considered an insult or loss of face; nor is it an indication of "no confidence." Our whole approach to research is different. We have no personal overtones. Your *ideas* are being looked at, not you yourself. To us the two are quite separate. This is the way our minds work. We are seeking facts; we are not challenging you as a person. So, too, even in social conversations you will find that people often argue, pick an idea apart, ask for your sources or challenge your conclusions. They do not mean to be rude; they are keenly interested and merely trying to explore the *idea* in greater depth.

CONTROLLING NATURE

Many people in the world—most Asians, for example—seek to "discover Man's place in Nature." Americans try instead to 'control" nature. We speak of "harnessing" a river, "conquering" space, "taming" the wilderness. Asians (and many others) think more in terms of "compromise," "consensus," or "harmony." Americans believe anything can be done "if we just put our minds to it." Americans say: "The difficult can be done today; the impossible takes a little longer." So the searching, challenging— often arrogant—mind goes to work. Nothing is left to Allah, to Fate, or to Time to solve.

Fortunately, we are beginning to realize that Man cannot "control" Nature. We are coming to understand how we have wasted and spoiled and polluted for the sake of transient gain. We are worried now about the nation's resources, the ugliness, the "urban blight." You will read about this in our newspapers and hear it discussed widely wherever you go.

ORDER AND INTIATIVE

In many nations the very fabric of life depends on planning and order; complex formal relationships are preordained by custom. People coming from such traditional countries often consider American ideals of personal initiative or freedom (including the freedom to disagree) and our whole economic system of free enterprise to be chaotic, uncontrolled, and confusing. Some even see them as leading to "anarchy." To them such freedoms are too "loose," too "unstructured" to be comfortable.

At every level this country is working through enormous changes, therefore life in America today does feel "chaotic." The very fiber of the nation is being ripped apart and rewoven; deep-lying social attitudes are undergoing tremendous questioning. Is there any *real* morality? Why has the nation never given black people full opportunity? What school subjects are relevant and needed in this fast-paced and technological world? Is marriage outmoded? What is the role of women in today's society?

As you live and work here, you will realize that thousands of Americans are beginning to turn away from the cities in disgust, seeking rural values and quieter lives; much of the old "establishment" is being cast aside; political patterns are shifting; labor-management relationships are being reworked; highly advanced skills that recently were in demand are suddenly no longer needed. The nation is in almost total flux on every front.

This is not necessarily bad for any country. Profound searchings and basic shifts may be useful and necessary. If we handle them well, the nation may come out of them wiser, more moderate, stronger. The only thing certain at this time is that the whole country is in the process of much violent ferment, questioning, and change.

These are, therefore, interesting, lively, stimulating, but also confusing times in American history. Those who come to the country during this transitional period must try hard to understand, rather than pass judgement too quickly on the confusion that they will certainly feel and see.

TRUTH OR COURTESY?

Just as our degree of individual freedom seems "loose" and therefore uncomfortable to many foreign visitors, foreign attitudes toward truth seem "loose" and uncertain to Americans.

In many countries people will tell you what they think you want to hear, whether or not it is true. To them, this implies politeness. To Americans, it is considered misleading—even dishonest—to distort facts on purpose, however kind the motive. The point is—our priorities are different; in the United States truth has a higher priority than politeness. We are taught from babyhood that "Honesty is the best policy." Elsewhere, courtesy, honor, family loyalty, "machismo" or many other values might come far ahead of honesty if one were listing priorities.

But with us, trust and truth are of paramount importance. If we say of a man, "You cannot trust him." this is one of the most damning statements that can be made about him.

In view of such profound differences in values, it is natural that misunderstandings and irritations often occur, especially in exact areas such as the negotiation of contracts. A Mexican has said, "With us a business deal is like a courtship." Americans lack this grace, but on the other hand you can count on their word. You know where you are with them; except in advertising, they will not be "whispering sweet nothings" that they do not mean in order to make you feel desirable!

"How far is it to the next village?" the American asks a man standing by the edge of the road. In some countries, because the man realizes that the traveler is tired and eager to reach his destination, he will politely say "Just down the road." He thinks this is more encouraging, gentler, and therefore the wanted answer. So the American drives on through the night, getting more and more angry, feeling "tricked." He thinks the man deliberately lied to him, for obviously he must have known the distance quite well.

Had conditions been reversed, the American would feel he was "cheating" the driver if he implied the next town was close when he knew it was really 15 miles further on. Although, he, too, would be sympathetic to the weary driver, he would say "You have a good way to go yet; it is at least 15 more miles." The driver might be disappointed, but he would know what to expect.

This oft-repeated question of accuracy versus courtesy leads to many misunderstandings between people of different cultures. If you are aware of the situation in advance, it is sometimes easier to recognize the problem.

PERSONAL PROGRESS AND JOB-HOPPING

In many parts of the world, personal influence is almost essential in getting ahead. One needs a "godfather," a "sponsor." Here that is not true. Naturally all people use influence sometimes, but one rarely advances far on that basis alone in the United States. Here traits which lead to success are generally considered to be the willingness to work hard (at any kind of job), scholarship or skill, initiative, an agreeable and outgoing personality. In other words even in the realm of personal progress, this is a "do-it-yourself"society. By and large, success is neither inherited nor bestowed. This means, therefore, that our employment practices are different from those in many other countries.

In some nations it is considered disloyal to quit a job; deep reciprocal loyalties exist between employee and employer (recipient and "patron" in many cases); lifelong job security and family honor are frequently involved.

This is not true in the United States. "Job-hopping" is part of our constant mobility. We consider it a "right" to be able to better ourselves, to move upward, to jump from company to company if we can keep qualifying for more responsible (and therefore better) jobs.

This interchangeability of personnel seems unreasonable to some members of foreign nations. Where are our roots? How can we be so cold and inhuman? "We act," some say, "as if we were dealing with machines, not humans." They do not understand that a great many Americans *like* to move about. New jobs present new challenges, new opportunities, new friends, new experiences—often a new part of the country.

The employer may be quite content too. Perhaps he has had the best of that man's thinking; a new person may bring in fresh ideas, improved skills, or new abilities. Then, too, a newcomer will probably start at a lower salary for he will have no seniority. Hopping is so readily accepted here, in fact, that a good man may bounce back and forth among two or three corporations, being welcomed back to his original company more than once through his career, each time at a different level.

WEALTH, PRIVILEGE, AND THE MASS MARKET

Status symbols such as cars, color television sets, and swimming pools often confuse visitors to the States. Most Arabs, Latins and Africans, for example, are accustomed to a two-class system in which privilege exists only when accompanied by wealth. Classes are polarized and there are just two: rich and poor. A luxury market supplies a small number of expensive goods for the rich; everyone else does without.

In the United States this is not true. Because in our economy we operate on the basis of a mass market, blue-collar workers, miners, farmers, even people on welfare own goods that represent great wealth elsewhere. In terms of hours-of-work, the cost for such luxuries here is low. A visitor from Ecuador, for example, assumes that the owner of a car in the United States is as rich as an

Ecuadorian car owner has to be. Actually this is not the case; stenographers high school students, or janitors can and do buy cars, trips abroad,all kinds of luxuries on the installment plan—as do most other people. The costs over a reasonable period of time are not prohibitive in terms of their wages.

This difference can be perplexing for the visitor who, understandably, interprets wealth in his terms, thinking a Cadillac car and mink coat *must* indicate high class and therefore education. As a result he expects to find that the owner possesses the cultural level that he thinks accompanies leisure. In America this is not necessarily so. Quick money comes from all kinds of sources; "rags to riches" is still a common U.S. occurrence. The opulent money spender is not necessarily either educated or cultured—in fact, he is usually neither!

CLASS

America likes to claim that is is a "classless" society. Maximum wages, a high standard of living, mass-produced clothing, purposefully casual speech, and the wide use of first names all combine to give the nation an affluent, classless appearance, especially to newcomers. But, under this professedly equal "veneer," the United States is, in fact, markedly segmented into neighborhoods, residential areas, and ghettos—right and wrong sides of town.

It is important to remember, however, that in the United States it is easy for people to move from one class to another on their own merits, and to become an accepted part of a new setting. To do so, a person needs enough energy, determination, and ability to make a real success of *something*. He can start as a salesman, factory hand, riveter, taxi driver, trainee, or bank teller. . . Americans love—and many are themselves living proof of—the "Self-made Man." You can hear these stories all around you if you ask people about their youth: the women whose father was a miner but she is now a leading journalist; the man who put himself through school by selling brushes but now is president of the brush company. . . .These are the dramatic stories, but, for every one who gets right to the top there are thousands of others who, less dramatically but nonetheless truly, move many steps beyond their parents on the social and economic ladder.

This constant flow of people from one social level to another indicates that both the word and the idea of "class" mean something so different in the United States from most other countries that the whole subject needs to be considered here. Not only is this nation made up of highly diverse ethnic, racial, and social strands, as we have noted, but, as we have also said, its inhabitants are enormously mobile geographically. People shift and move across its length and breadth to a remarkable degree. One statistical study reports that one out of five families moves every three years!

This ceaseless mixing and merging in new communities, this repeated adjustment to new environments and new people, is an important factor in trying to understand the baffling questioning of class in America. The do-it-yourself, independent, questioning American personality is another factor.

In many lands a man's social position is still a group matter, shared with his family, his wider group of relatives or clan, perhaps even his whole village or district. Not so the American's. In the United States, position in society is, to a large degree, personal rather than family or group.

Before World War II, family feeling was strong in America too. Uncles, aunts, grandparents, and children of all ages vacationed with one another, came together for holiday festivities, and were a closely knit unit. But as technology takes hold in any nation, social patterns are bound to change. The mathematician or scientist suddenly is in great demand and moves faster than his colleagues into new prominence; technological jobs and new plants require firms to send people to new areas, removing them from stable family ties; more and more people settle in small houses in urban areas where grandparents and other family members can no longer share space.

The same shift is beginning to take place in other countries. Nowadays a man who can read and understand the newspaper or fix a tractor may, and often does, take over from the traditional leader. Technology puts a premium on youth which better understands electronics, computers, atomic energy, and the space age. Young people move ahead, starting new families in new ways. As people learn complicated modern skills, their wages rise; the "onward and upward" ferment becomes more and more widespread; traditional classes and position are torn apart by the force of twentieth-century demands.

Frequently it is just one member of a family who surges ahead; becoming president of a university, head of a firm, or a well-known member of government—while the rest of the family remains in modest jobs in a modest environment. When this happens, many Americans feel no psychological commitment either to their relatives or to their community. Some, of course, maintain strong ties of affection and loyalty, but for many, new frontiers beckon. They may come back now and then to their former environment, but many move away, never to return.

Most nations derive considerable security from basic, stable, lasting human ties. For them each person is embedded in a lifelong and supportive network of family and community relationships. However, the American, seemingly self-sufficient but rootless, rarely can take his own position for granted. Throughout life, most Americans keep on making new alliances, losing them, moving on to others. For most people "class" is a competitve and changing thing. Class edges, therefore, are blurred.

Studies show that four out of five Americans when asked, describe themselves as "middle class." In most other countries higher percentages of people tend to define "class" more closely and therefore describe themselves either as "upper class" or "lower class"; many even subdivide "middle" into either "upper or lower middle." Nowadays few Americans think in terms of "lower-middle-upper." Especially among the young, this former system of stereotyping is breaking down. Race, ethnic background, region, or "counterculture" are replacing the word "class," and the whole social structure is undergoing profound changes. Much of our so-called "middle class" has been migrating to suburbia and been replaced in the cities by new combinations of ethnic and racial groups.

"Success" can be defined as that which gives a man (or woman) more power than he possessed before. It can be won through skill, intelligence, leadership, sometimes sheer perseverance, regardless of birth. In the American scene "success" has normally been accompanied by increased financial rewards. The "upward-moving man," therefore, has traditionally found himself associating with first one and then another "success level," with its accompanying money level.

As a result, "class" in the United States is determined both by a person's job and pattern of consumption. Since "class" is a flexible, competitive matter, people try to make their position clear by visible and recognizable symbols such as cars, houses, clubs, vacations, and so on. As someone has said, "Middle-class America progresses from the little Cape Cod to the split-level with the dropped living room, and on to the larger house with a panelled den." Those considered "below" are often subtly rejected by those who have risen on the social and economic ladder. Racial and ethnic discrimination should be seen, in this country, against the background of a much broader but less discussed tendency of many Americans to exclude one another—of any color—through fear of losing their own place. Much that is thought to be racial prejudice here is in fact as much cultural prejudice. "Poor Whites" in the South, for example fear the rise of Blacks on an educational and job threat basis, as well as merely for skin color. The feeling of job threat plays a large part in the widespread blockage of Black membership in unions.

Our youth is in the process of trying to work out new goals and values. Many of them have been deeply disillusioned by the Vietnam War, Watergate (in its broadest sense), repeated exposure to graft and wrong-doing in high places—both governmental and business.

Many young people find their idealism under great strain. They see and hear about corruption and extortion in the world around them and see—via the medium of television—injustice in the courts and in daily life—not just in the U.S. but worldwide. They become cynical early.

Many of them look on life differently from their elders: "Suddenly to be white is no big deal . . . to be a policeman or a judge is only being a border guard on middle-class turf." A doctor is "an exploiter of middle-class illness" and a businessman "a exploiter of middle-class greed." College to many of them becomes "a middle-class union card leading into the middle-class managerial net." Service in the army is no longer seen as an honorable duty but as "professional killing."

Many of these, the unhappy sceptics, are the ones who "pop the pills" as they say, or sniff glue, take to alcohol, muggings, break-ins or stealing cars.

Others are complacent. They are affluent, comfortable, life for them is easy. Why worry about other people's problems?

The majority—as is always the case—falls between the two extremes. They work hard and feel a strong sense of purpose; they start earning money early to help put themselves through college; they care about the environment, or work with computers or advanced scientific experiments; they run, compete hard in tennis or baseball; they backpack around the world to learn about its people.

The attitudes of youth, various shifting status symbols, and many new social trends are complex and difficult even for Americans to interpret. No one will expect you to do so. However, if you can understand that in America social position is not a stable, inherited factor, you will comprehend much about the nation.

Whenever any society is mobile and competitive, tensions are inevitable. You will be acutely aware of social tensions in American life. Could it be, however, that stress and strain are needed—anywhere—for full national vitality?

In order to fulfill its function, a watch or clock must be both under tension and in motion. Might the same be true also for a nation—or a person?

ETHNIC DIFFERENCES

A cherished American myth is that this nation is a great melting pot, a haven for the oppressed.

In fact, as we said earlier, it is not a "melting pot" at all. This is one of the deep reasons underlying the fast-shifting social patterns of today. This country was founded almost wholly by "WASP's"— White, Anglo-Saxon, mostly Protestant people. As one discovers by reading American history books, they have never truly recognized the contributions made by any other incoming groups—Negro, Mexican, Italian, Japanese, Chinese, Irish. Members of these groups have worked hard to become "assimilated," where possible —that is, to take on "WASP" characteristics and become a part of the white American culture. But for those with racial features which could always be recognized, assimilation has not been possible. As the years have passed, the proportion of WASP's to other Americans has radically changed. WASP's are now a marked minority in many parts of the country. The new majorities, having been rejected over the years, understandably are turning back to their own ethnic and racial backgrounds, seeking their own pride and identity out of their own past histories. The largest and most noticeable of these groups is, of course, the 11 percent of the nation who are black.

The whole question of their changing role in American society has been so played up in the world's headlines that visitors to our shores often expect to find police dogs, mob scenes, and bar fights everywhere when they arrive. They are likely to be surprised when instead they see Blacks and Whites working side by side in offices, factories, schools, and institutions in cities across the country. Not everyone realizes that the majority of Blacks are urban, congregated in and around a relatively small number of U.S. cities. Large areas of agricultural America have almost no Blacks at all, sometimes from bigotry but often also from Black choice.

Many dark-skinned people arrive here fearing personal attack or expecting various degrees of apartheid. Slights, insults, and narrow-minded boycotting do still take place unfortunately, especially in the crucial areas of housing, schools, and jobs. There are still frictions and outbursts. School equality is, to our shame, still a dream and not a reality. There are still too many areas of the country where black people do not enjoy the full range of opportunities available to Whites.

However, the overwhelming majority of Americans are finally working, studying, and sharing facilities together, including restaurants, bathing areas, concert halls, parks, and rest rooms. This was not true even a few years ago, so progress is slowly being made. You will be able to observe this as soon as your plane lands. You will see it in the airport, in the public buses and trains, in movie houses and eating places, in department stores and libraries, in offices and plants. Real friendships between the races, full trust, easy social encounters are still far too rare. However, even in this—the slowest area of progress—barriers are gradually breaking down, especially among the young.

BLACK AMERICANS

Because the world press has concentrated mostly on the negative scene with little reference to any kind of progress, newcomers may at first be surprised at the economic range they will find among black Americans. They will see many Blacks who own good cars, fine homes, stylish clothes. Colleges are opening the way to better jobs. Black executives, judges, and professors are no longer rare. More and more Blacks are buying houses and apartments in formerly all-white areas and sending their children to school with their white counterparts. As everyone knows, this varies by locality and progress is slow, but in the past twenty years there has been much forward motion. Those coming from abroad will find a wide gamut of acceptance, but much of it will depend on their own educational background and personality. They need not fear violence or personal attack because of race (though unfortunately both black and white people are too often attacked for other reasons in our cities these days). Black visitors who look for slights and insults will find them; those who do not will encounter much good will, acceptance, and friendship, among both Blacks and Whites.

Writes a young African studying in rural America: "Most girls are white. Some do not mind dating Blacks, some do. Some have never seen a Black and are sort of scared; but I get along well and am happy". This is probably a fair picture of interracial dating across much of this wide land. The Black community often feels equally separatist; many do not want to date Whites either.

HISPANIC AMERICANS

The fastest growing minority in the United States is that of the Hispanic Americans. It includes people of Mexican heritage, living primarily in the west (including the southwest and midwest), Puerto Ricans, concentrated largely along the east coast especially in New York but moving in greater numbers into the midwest, and Cuban-Americans, the newest group, many of whom have settled in Florida. The total number of Hispanic Americans is expected to reach twenty million before the end of the 1980's. They add a special blend of Spanish, Indian and African cultures to the national fabric, bringing with them the heritage of the Caribbean and varied parts of Central and South America. A Mexican writes of the Hispanic heritage in the United States:

"We explored and charted areas and regions which, for example, later became Florida, Georgia, Louisiana and Missouri. We were the first cowboys. Through our ancient knowledge of irrigation we made an oasis out of desert areas in Arizona and California. We built many of the waterways, railroads, and charted many of the original trails that became the highways of the southwest." (Gilbert G. Pompa, Director of Community Relations Service, Pontiac, Michigan—taken from a speech.)

Their numbers are now so great that you will find bilingual
(Spanish-English) signs, instructions and even bilingual schools in
many parts of the country. Bilingualism, especially in the schools, is
becoming an issue of some significance in the U.S. Efforts to
provide public school instruction in a student's first language (not
only Spanish but other languages as well) are felt by many to subvert
the melting pot concept of American Society and sow the seeds of
disunity. You will probably encounter this debate, especially in the
newspapers where national policy on the subject is discussed.

TAX EVASION

Naturally nobody enjoys paying taxes wherever they live. However, where governments back massive welfare, housing, or school
programs, and build miles of highways, they must have money. Tax
evasion in the United States is considered "fraud" and is looked
upon as a serious offense. Computers check the tax returns of rich
and poor alike; audits from the Internal Revenue Service are widespread. When rich evaders are caught, they are subject to the same
penalty rates that apply to the poor. This is not true in all countries
—as many readers well know. But here newspapers feature the
action as "front-page scandal" when a wealthy, highly placed
person or a corporation is found evading the law. Our legal basis is
that "private interests are subordinate to public good." Since tax
evasion is regarded as affecting the welfare of the entire community
and nation, it is looked upon as a major offense—not worth trying!

MAJORITY-MINORITY COOPERATION

The fact that a minority will peacefully accept the outcome of a
hotly contested vote and the idea of cooperation among bitter
political adversaries are difficult concepts for many visitors to
understand. Some people fear what they call the "tyranny" of the
majority. "How does a minority ever get heard?" they ask.

Such people may be interested in attending a town meeting in a small American town. Here anyone may listen as citizens argue hotly, fiercely, loud, and long over some local issue. Finally the vote is called and counted. As the visitor watches, he may see speakers who were bitterly opposed shake hands and offer each other a lift home! The loser does not feel dejected. He will begin straightway gain to line up new support (often called lobbying) or he will work on the same issue through some other channel. His loss is taken in good grace: "I have to work harder to build a bigger majority" is the way he is likely to react. Americans start early to learn the system. From first grade onward in school, they campaign, vote, and elect class committees and even "officers" from among their own number. This is part of the reason for the "Fruit Juice Committee," "Goldfish Feeding Committee," Black-board Cleaning Committee" or similar rather ridiculous-sounding committees found even as early as in kindergarten classes. The process of voting and the idea of "majority-minority" soon become familiar to Americans. They learn to accept defeat and work toward another day—to live, in other words, within our type of governmental structure.

THE RELATIONSHIP BETWEEN STATE AND NATION

Those who come from lands where the State is supreme find personal initiative in politics baffling; "grass-roots democracy" seems to them chaotic; the relationship among our localities, states, and the nation is hard for them to understand.

To an American the word "State" means one of 50 geographic and fairly autonomous units, united by our rather loose Federal Government. But to a Frenchman, a Russian, a Syrian, a Korean, or to many others, the word "State" means a strongly centralized national government with absolute powers far beyond those held by our federal authorities. To those accustomed to any form of "Strong Man (or Strong Committee) rule," be they from South America, Asia, Africa, or elsewhere, strongly centralized governmental power is normal and comfortable. Such people expect a leader to act decisively, quickly, and alone. They do not understand the American preference for compromise, committee decision, or consultation with many "lesser" people, some of whom may, in fact, be the leader's enemies. Long delays or legal "quibbling" while our government "tests the winds of public opinion" are often mistakenly interpreted as meaning that our President does not really care about the question or is, in fact, not sincere in his stand.

Visitors often ask: "How can a local legislature defy *national* authority?" How, for example, can there still be segregation in American schools when almost 20 years ago the nation's Supreme Court ruled that it was unconstitutional? Does this mean, they ask:

1) that there is no strength in the "Central" government? (If so, why do they not call out the army to enforce their ruling and show strength?)

2) that the whole system is a sham—a show of empty words? Is it all hypocrisy?

Because of its enormous size and the great variety of its people, the United States has developed a system that allows for doing things gradually (although, in fact, there have been occasions when troops have been called out to enforce a ruling). In constructing a large building, one allows spaces for the stretching and shrinking of metals. We operate on that same principle. Ideas proceed at different speeds in different areas and at different levels of society; an issue packed with emotion in some areas takes longer to be resolved there than elsewhere. So the American system was devised with "spaces." Time must be allowed, winds of opinion must be tested, in order to preserve the diversity of this enormous country, while at the same time giving it a basic framework of unity. It is cumbersome and often slow, but precisely because there is leeway, the country has remained a unit despite its share of searing critical differences through the years. If these differences had been met head-on by absolute governmental decree, the nation would almost surely have been fragmented long ago. Many countries face such possible fragmentation within their own borders today because "leeway," gradualism, public opinion, and other safeguards have not been built into their system.

Since public opinion is so vitally important in America, our leaders *must* work within its boundaries. To do so, they must keep consulting, compromising, conferring, and "feeling the pulse" of the nation. Those who are accustomed to public institutions being the instruments of a Central Government naturally look for a unified "line" somewhere in the United States; they do not find it. They assume a country *reflects* government policy. In fact, in the United States it is more usual for public opinion to *direct* government policy. The American people, for example, demanded withdrawal from Vietnam long before the government took that stand. Black and white citizens marched and struggled and demonstrated together for civil rights so long and hard and steadily that the Supreme Court ruling on desegregation finally resulted; it was not initiated by the government but by the people themselves.

What newcomers need to understand is that we Americans recognize differences and allow leeway among: 1) the law; 2) policy; and 3) the actual situation. These three factors often pull and tug just as a ship creaks and strains when its hull meets conflicting winds and waters. But there are two important points: 1) It remains a ship and 2) It continues to move ahead, however slowly. It does this because it has play in its joints. Therefore it does not founder but can stay afloat even under heavy stress.

Let us look again at the deeply divisive national problem of civil rights:

1) *The Law:* By federal law there are now neither legal nor constitutional discriminations against Blacks.

2) *Policy:* The federal policy is: Discrimination is illegal and should be phased out "with all possible speed."

3) *The Facts:* All too slowly, with uneven pace, sometimes two steps forward and one step back, faster in some states than in others, America is gradually moving toward a real equality.

The country is struggling with countless other serious issues that occur at national, state, local, and personal levels. It will undoubtedly continue to struggle with all of them for a long time, gradually working out accommodations and resolving various kinds of problems. Despite all kinds of deep regional, emotional, and personal differences, the nation will be kept on course throughout this process by the law of the land.

It is often difficult for those from highly centralized nations to understand, but the fact is that final power really *does* lie in the hands of the people in the United States. This is true whether one speaks of political, economic, or social power. Americans distrust and will not long tolerate being "pushed" by a Strong Man or a strong government. They want to keep power decentralized; they like it that way. Social changes, therefore (such as civil rights, divorce laws, equality of pay for women, abortion laws), are debated long, hard, and often terribly slowly at state level. National law reflects many *state* differences and attitudes. Change comes heartbreakingly slowly after endless debate. But those changes which finally become the law of the land do so eventually with the work, the thought, and the consent of a nationwide majority. Most laws, therefore, remain stable once achieved.

AMERICANS THINK FROM SMALL TO LARGE

Americans tend to move from the specific and small to the general and large. We have just seen an example of this in the fact that they progress from personal and local issues to the state and finally to the nation—not the other way around.

Many other people, including Italians, Russians, Japanese and most South Amer cans, tend to move the other way: it is more comfortable for them to start with a general or universal idea and then narrow it down to specific facts. The differences between these two approaches is subtle and usually unrecognized in daily life. Actually, however, it lies at the root of many everyday misunderstandings and irritations among peoples of different cultures.

Let us take as simple an example as the addressing of envelopes. Many who start with the general and move to the particular begin the address with the country; then they write the prefecture (or province, department, county, or state); then the city; the district of the city; the street; and finally the number of the actual house. In the United States people start with the smallest item, namely the number of the house. The address then moves on to the larger divisions: the street, the town, the state, and finally the country.

This totally opposite approach to thinking affects many negotiations, plans, or attitudes, whether we recognize it or not. If an Indian, Japanese, or Mexican asks an American about an overall goal, a basic theory, or a principle, he often feels buried under detail in the answer he gets. He is confused by a flood of statistics or a long description of *method* before he hears any overall purpose or plan. People say: "Ask an American the time and he tells you how to build the clock!" Americans, on the other hand, feel equally frustrated when they ask for a specific fact or detail but then are subjected to 20 minutes of theory, philosophy, or universality without a single concrete fact!

Neither of us can—or will want to—change our lifetime patterns of thought. However, it may help us both if we recognize the possibilities of difference along these lines.

Chapter 4

Doing Business in the United States

FOREIGN BUSINESS IS GROWING RAPIDLY

The combined sales of the 100 largest foreign investing companies in the U.S. increased by a staggering 40% in the two years between 1977 and 1979, and the number has continued to increase steadily. In 1980 South Africa proved to be the largest financial investor in the U.S., controlling about $19.2 billion in sales. The Netherlands and the U.K. follow as second largest investors—and Germany next. New to the list of the top 100 foreign investors are 12 banking and finance and insurance companies—the largest, The Hong Kong Shanghai Banking Corp., from Hong Kong. (*Forbes,* April 1979 and July 1980). The number of Latin American companies engaged in business here is growing steadily, often through third country holding companies.

Why are so many firms coming to the U.S.? There are many reasons. One of the greatest attractions, of course, is a market of over 200 million consumers with a high average per capita income. In addition, with the devalued dollar the cost of American labor has declined markedly, relative to many foreign labor costs. Some firms seeking to avoid bureaucratic and/or political pressures at home, find the U.S. a politically stable environment in which to work. Many hope to be able to continue selling to the American market even if the U.S. government restricts imports further, or if major price changes occur due to currency fluctuations. Many foreigners are attracted by U.S. technology, its modern management methods, its labor saving and mass production techniques.

U.S. GOVERNMENT POLICY

The general policy of the U.S. government has been to admit and

42

treat foreign capital on an equal basis with domestic capital. Except in a few sensitive areas (such as communications, defense, and coastal shipping) there are few federally imposed limitations on foreign investment in the U.S. However, under their own constitutions, some *states* have considerable power in regulating investment that falls under their jurisdiction. State laws need to be carefully understood in any matters of acquisition. Every state also has its own tax system, regulating the systems of all localities within its borders. From state to state, matters such as the availability of skilled labor, requirements for pollution control, and the like vary widely.

In 1974 a federal Committee on Foreign Investment in the United States was established to monitor the impact of direct foreign investment in the country. At present, the U.S. branches or subsidiaries (above a certain size) of foreign parent companies must register by filing quarterly reports with the U.S. Department of Commerce. There are, however, no exchange controls; loans, income and share capital can all be repatriated to home countries.

New arrivals doing business in the United States will find that U.S. economic strength has traditionally been built on the private sector of business. Monopolies, cartels and other restraints of trade are prevented by law. Some industries—such as banking, insurance, transportation and utilities—are government regulated but, although there are many complaints about government paperwork, there is, in fact, far less federal regulation than in many other highly develoned economies.

Much of the required paperwork results from the close scrutiny by a wide range of government agencies over such matters as taxation, consumer protection, food and drugs, environmental controls, equal labor opportunities, etc. Many such protections have, in fact, been added as a result of the pressures and lobbying of concerned citizens.

LABOR UNIONS

A new arrival will find considerable disparity in the whole trade union picture, due in large degree to the enormous size of the country and the diversity of American workers. There are several national unions but most of these operate through regional or local chapters. The extent to which labor is organized at all varies a good deal, depending both on the type of industry and the region of the country. The amount of power a given union can exert also varies considerably. The most highly unionized industries are mining, construction (including all its subdivisions, such as electrical work, plumbing, etc.), manufacturing, printing, and public utilities. Among the least unionized are agriculture, the professions, banking, and insurance.

Contracts between management and unions are for fixed periods of time, enforceable by law. "Wildcat" or unauthorized strikes are rare; authorized strikes usually take place as a contract expires, almost as part of the bargaining process. Very often both labor and management know about them in advance and plan accordingly.

Currently, organized labor is under considerable attack from well-organized and well-financed business organizations determined to reduce union power. In recent years organized labor has had great political power, working to elect those candidates across the country who would represent their interests in the legislative process. Business began adopting labor's election strategies and developing strong political action committees a few years ago. They are now working hard to support business-oriented candidates at every level of government, national, state and local.

WOMEN IN THE WORKING WORLD

During the second quarter of 1979 American women passed a milestone. More than 50% of those over 16 years of age are now reported to be in the labor force, full or part-time. Women hold more than 42% of all jobs in the nation and their influx into the job market continues at a rapid pace. It is expected that by the end of the 1980's, 70 to 80% of the female population will be part of the nation's paid work force. Most, of course, are still employed in jobs traditionally filled by women: clerical, sales, production and service. Growing numbers, however, are moving into those higher level, well paid positions and professions once reserved almost exclusively for men. Analysts expect this trend to continue, in no small measure because inflation and rising costs make it necessary for women to work, and also because more and more women choose to work at careers outside the home.

In many families, it now requires two pay-checks to meet the high costs of even a "moderate" standard of living. The poor have always struggled to "make ends meet," now the more affluent are also feeling the pinch.

With the decline in the birthrate, the high divorce and separation rate, and the subsequent rush of women into the workplace, it is hard to find the once "typical" family of father at work, mother in her apron at home, and two children in the nest. This profile accounts for less than 15% of all American families, hard though that may be to believe. Today it is far more common for families to be headed by a single parent or for both parents to be working, managing their lives in ways unpredictable even twenty years ago.

"For us it works out well," said one father who splits house and childcare with his wife, an airline hostess. "I know the children much better than I did, the quality of time we all spend together is better, the children have adjusted easily, and working has added an important new dimension to my wife's life."

Not all families are so liberated. The day to day management of families can, in fact, be quite difficult for working women who normally do most of the household tasks, fitting them into weekends and evenings after a full day at work.

Society is groping for ways to adjust to the rush of women into the work force. Much research is being done on the impact of this trend on the stability of families. Interestingly, to date it has been shown that there is little relationship between employed women and divorce. In fact busy wives and higher double incomes seem to be a factor towards greater stability. Social observers who formerly predicted the decline of family life in the U.S.A. are now revising their predictions. They say there are signs that the divorce rate is no longer climbing. More people are getting married later—with greater maturity. It is teenage marriages which still are the most likely to end in divorce.

America is dealing with turbulent social change on all fronts. There is growing recognition that the family is a diverse and complex entity, the "traditional family" being only one form of it. In these days of steady financial pressure, it is not likely ever to revert to its old traditional form.

Society is seeking—and needs to do more—to help working mothers and fathers raise their children successfully within a new framework of family patterns.

JOB SHARING

A new direction, resulting from changing values and lifestyles, is the increase in part-time or job-shared work. Growing numbers of people are reducing their income and job responsibilities in order to gain time for other pursuits—sharing child-care responsibilities or developing fuller lives for themselves. They may want to learn new skills, study or conduct research, take part in sports, or simply live with less pressure. Some aim to avoid entry into higher tax brackets. Many who are old enough to retire prefer to remain in the mainstream of life by working a few hours a day or a few days a week.

Twenty-one per cent of the labor force is now working on a part-time basis, according to the U.S. Bureau of Labor Statistics. Many jobs have been divided—or totally restructured—so that two people can work on what was formerly one full-time job. In other situations, people create a new way of working together, sharing different aspects of the responsibility. Sometimes both work full-time during peak periods but then merely cover for each other in less busy times.

Rather than a deterioration of the work ethic, this interest in part-time work reflects a reordering of priorities—a recognition that people do not have to pursue each interest that they have individually only during particular periods in their lives. Adjustments can be made to accommodate all of them, education, work, family responsibilities, leisure, at the same time though at varying levels of intensity.

Furthermore, communities may benefit from the additional time that is devoted to worthwhile activities, such as volunteering at a hospital or making improvements on one's home, and from the increase in the number of available jobs.

There is sense to the trend; *all* may benefit when the system accommodates people who need to work but do not need (or want) to do so full-time.

THE "SUNNING OF AMERICA"

Like a slow, viscous flow of lava, the population of the United States is steadily moving toward the south and southwest. Expectations are that within twenty years the combined populations of southern and western states will have doubled—to 150 million people, or 56% of the entire population. Some people call this the "sunning of America" because almost two-thirds of the nation's growth since 1970 has occured in the south (or "Sunbelt").

The fastest growing centers during this decade have been Houston, Texas; Tampa/St. Petersburg, Florida; and Phoenix, Arizona. The city of Atlanta in Georgia has also grown to the point that it is planning to widen some of its four-lane highways to ten lanes; Denver, Colorado and the region around Dallas, Texas, are among other areas that are growing rapidly. In the same period, New York City has lost more than 6% of its population; many other cities in the east and north have also shown noticeable declines.

Since migrating workers tend to be young and among the more qualified, the north and east are losing some of their most able youth. The south and west, while gaining from this migration, are having to deal with the major problems of providing housing, education, and other services needed by the flood of new residents.

Economic activity is being decentralized away from the regions of earliest industrialization: New England, the Middle Atlantic States, and the Great Lakes area. Interestingly, large numbers of foreign firms are taking up much of the slack in these "Frost Belt" states as they find plants in the north empty and available for purchase with skilled workers nearby looking for jobs. An equalization of income has occurred across all eight regions of the country. The southeast no longer has the lowest regional per capita income level nor does the far west boast of having the highest.

As the population moves, there follows a reapportionment of government representation also. For the first time in United States history the south and west will soon hold half the seats in Congress. The nation's "center of gravity" has already reached the Mississippi River.

EVOLVING ATTITUDES TOWARD THE WORLD

Most Americans will take you as you are, as an individual. If you are pleasant, they will be too. However, you will be aware of a growing mood of "isolationism" across the country, a desire to withdraw into our own national concerns. The anguish of Vietnam started the trend. People felt that enormous numbers of young lives were lost with no gain for anyone, especially not for the Vietnamese. The whole tragedy seems to Americans to have been both senseless and bungled. Most people did not feel we should have been there in the first place and did not understand why we were.

Trauma over the U.S. hostages in Iran affected the nation deeply and has caused much soul-searching. Multiple kidnappings of American executives and the bombings of U.S. embassies in various parts of the world have given rise to further deep questioning and resentment. Anti-west and specifically anti-U.S. attitudes spreading throughout much of the world baffle the average American. This nation believes it has generously sent its young men, its own hard-earned dollars, and its technical experts abroad in an honest effort to help other nations. Other people may see U.S. efforts overseas differently but that is how they are perceived here. Americans do not understand why they have been rewarded with expressions of dislike—even hatred in some cases—directed toward their country.

Now Americans are reading reports of increasing numbers of foreigners "gaining control" over assets worth multi-million dollars in the U.S. They worry about foreigners owning property here but not being subject to our laws. "When we turn ownership of our heritage—our property and our resources—over to outside people we are giving them political power. That is the same thing as economic power; we should recognize it as such," said one concerned businessman. Unemployment is high; workers across the country worry about the predictability of foreign bosses. Few realize that the amount of U.S. money invested abroad in other people's countries is still about four times that of foreign money invested in the U.S. Still fewer have any understanding of the extent to which foreign money is then being reinvested again in the U.S., nor do they understand benefits derived from that investment.

In short, you will find Americans echoing exactly the same objections often voiced by people in other countries when firms from outside nations invest heavily in their economies.

However, most Americans stem from foreign roots and still feel the pull of old ties. As *individuals,* most people from abroad can expect to find a welcome even though "foreigners" in the abstract are seen by many as somewhat of a threat.

Furthermore, those many Americans who are profiting from foreign investment naturally welcome the trend and, therefore, will also welcome you. Foreign-owned plants are warmly received when they are established in areas where additional jobs, investments, and tax revenues are needed. Real estate dealers are, of course, delighted. Many large-scale farmers have also found their pot-of-gold. They sell land at great profit to a foreign buyer, then rent it back from him and continue to farm it. Both sides are happy. More than twenty states —and even some cities—are actively competing abroad for foreign

investment, offering special tax exemptions and favorable financing
to investors who settle in their areas. Those who come bringing
business with them are likely to perceive no mood of isolationism.

Chapter 5

Business Attitudes and Practices

Because people operate out of their heritage—influenced by their own historic pasts—there are necessarily a wide range of differing values, priorities, and behaviors that affect the way life is lived and business done around the world.

RISK-TAKERS AND EXPERIMENTERS

North Americans come from a frontier past. Many of them stemmed originally from rebel stock, being descended from people who braved terrible hardships in order to flee from other countries. Many of the early settlers were rebelling against conditions at home. They took great risks in order to establish a new land. That same element of seeking a new world has motivated wave after wave of immigrants who still come to the USA, leaving one world and seeking another. Vietnamese and Cuban refugees are among the latest groups to arrive on these shores in great numbers. The nation's frontier past, followed by these waves of sturdy immigrants, has brought a strong element of risk-taking into the nation's character. We are always looking beyond the next mountain range.

This exploratory element, coupled with what once seemed like limitless raw materials, has also made us profligate with materials. We scrap an idea, a machine, or a process in favor of something new if we consider the new to be better, faster, more heat-resistant, or whatever it may be. To people from countries where raw materials have always been scarce and where conserving has necessarily been a prime requisite, this is often jarring. The philosophy that it is "cheaper to scrap the old and replace it with something better" frequently seems to them to be both wasteful and foolhardy.

The American view is "no one stands still. If you are not moving ahead, you are falling behind." This attitude results in a nation of people geared, to a large degree, to researching, experimenting, and exploring. Most of its adventurer, rebel, or refugee stock came here only 200 years ago—or less. The country is young—perhaps a bit raw—but full of vitality.

TIME

There are two elements in life that Americans do, however, save carefully: time and labor.

We are "slaves to nothing but the clock" it has been said. Time is treated as if it were an almost tangible entity. Listen to the words associated with it: We *budget* it, *save* it, *waste* it, *steal* it, *kill* it, *cut* it, *account* for it; we also *charge* for it. It is a precious commodity. Many people have a rather acute sense of the shortness of each lifetime. Once the sands have run out of a person's hourglass, they cannot be replaced. We want every minute to count.

Since people value time highly, they resent someone else "wasting" it beyond a certain courtesy point. This affects the matter of patience. In the American system of values, patience is not a high priority. Many of us have what might be called "a short fuse." We begin to splutter and move restlessly about if we feel time is slipping away without some return—be this in terms of pleasure, work value, or rest. Those coming from lands where time is looked upon differently may find this matter of pace to be one of their most difficult adjustments in both business and daily life.

Many newcomers to the States will sorely miss the opening courtesies of a business call, for example. They will miss the welcoming tea or coffee that may habitually be served to office visitors in their own country. They may miss leisurely business chats in a cafe or coffee house.

Normally Americans do not assess their visitors in such relaxed surroundings over prolonged small talk; much less do they take them out for dinner, or a round on the golf course, while they develop a pre-business sense of trust and rapport. Rapport to most of us is less important than performance. We seek out credentials of past performance rather than evaluating a business colleague through social courtesies. Since we generally assess and probe professionally rather than socially, we start talking business very quickly.

Most Americans live in time segments by engagement calendars. These calendars may be divided into intervals as short as fifteen minutes. We often "give" a person two or three (or more) segments of our calendar, but in the business world we most always have other appointments following hard on the heels of whatever we are doing. Time is therefore always ticking in our inner ear.

As a result we work hard at the task of saving time. We produce a steady flow of labor saving devices; we communicate rapidly through telexes, phone calls, or memos rather than through personal contacts. These, though pleasant, take longer—especially through traffic-filled streets. We therefore save most personal visiting for after work hours or for social weekend gatherings.

To us the impersonality of electronic communication has little or no relation to the importance of the matter at hand. In some countries no major business is carried out without eye contact, requiring face to face conversation. In America, too, a *final* agreement will normally be signed in person; negotiation must, of course, be done across a table; major sales are finally consummated by individuals talking together. However, a high percentage of the various preparations leading up to these final stages is likely to have been done by voice, electronic device or mail.

As mentioned elsewhere, the U.S.A. is definitely a telephone country. This is due partly to the fact that telephone service is good here whereas postal service is poor. Partly it lies in the fact that the costs of secretarial labor, printing, and stamps are all soaring. Mostly, however, it is because the telephone is so quick. We like it. You can do your business and get your answer in a matter of moments. Furthermore, several people can confer together without moving from their desks, even in widely scattered locations. In a big country that, too, is important.

Some new arrivals will come from cultures where it is considered impolite to work too quickly. Unless a certain amount of time is allowed to elapse, it seems in their eyes as if the task were being considered insignificant, not worthy of substantial respect. Assignments are thus perceived to be given added weight by the passage of time. In the U.S.A., however, it is taken as a sign of competence to solve a problem, or fulfill a job successfully, with rapidity. Usually, the more important a task is, the more capital, energy, and attention will be poured into it in order to "get it moving."

LETTING EMOTIONS SHOW

We spoke above of "short fuses" for expressed irritation.

Many people in the U.S.A. make little effort to hide their emotions. This is a high-pressure country and, especially in the cities, most people live and work under a range of stresses; at home, at work, and in between. Most of us understand this fact and therefore make allowances for each other fairly readily. Our feelings are not easily hurt. "Joe is pretty uptight today," we will say, or "the meeting must have gone poorly," but we are not often deeply wounded by what is said in a fit of irritation. While no one likes to be subjected to irritation and there may be temporary return flare-ups, no one loses a great deal of "face" or "status" if he (she) evidences various ranges of emotion occasionally. Pleasure and excitement are equally readily expressed. On the whole most of us could not be described as a reserved, contained, disciplined people. Take us as we are: noisy, ebullient, often quick-tempered, but usually open—easy to read and understand. Most of us tell each other (and will tell you) exactly where we stand on any issue. You will find this has both good and bad aspects. Many may find this to be an area of real adjustment when they first encounter the American business world.

DIRECTNESS

Closely related to the need to "get on with the job without delay" is another widespread American characteristic, namely that of *directness* (sometimes also called Bluntness—see page 27). Again commonly used expressions indicate our emphasis:

> call a spade a spade
> don't beat around the bush
> put your cards on the table
> get down to brass tacks
> let the chips fall where they may
> or (more colloquially) "tell it like it is"

It is quite normal for us to jump right into a subject and say exactly what is on our minds. We often do not couch our comments in carefully gentle phrases to save a person's face or to allow for his "personalismo." We are not likely to withdraw from a clear cut confrontation between two issues; in fact we often purposefully separate opposing points out from the mainstream of thought to examine and discuss, rather than minimizing them. We are often like metronomes, separating our judgments into two clearly differentiated "beats;" a thing *is* or it *isn't*; it is *extroverted* or *introverted; black* or *white; developed* or *underdeveloped; good* or *bad*. Generally speaking, we are not a country given to grays, to compromises, to easy melds. We are like a banana—our skin is either on or it is off, whereas much of the world is more like an onion: one skin covers another and another and another, so one can have different depths, different layers; a number of varying truths can all be true at once.

The opposite of "calling a spade a spade" is *indirection*. Many of the world's people do their best to avoid confrontations. They talk around and around a point, making the edges more gentle, leaving easy leeway for retreats or changes of view on either side, showing their sense of respect for the other person by avoiding direct denials or negatives. Rather than saying a shipment **must** go out tomorrow for example, and meeting the reply: "it is **impossible** for it to go out tomorrow—for this and this reason" (confrontation) the same conversation (saving face) might go like this in an "indirect" country:

Manager: "I certainly hope this shipment can go out no later
         than tomorrow, for these and these reasons;"
Aide: "I think we may have a few problems; it may be a
         little bit difficult; but we will try our best."

Both know from that answer that it is unlikely to go out
tomorrow. However, the fact is not laid out on the line directly; no
one will lose face whether it does or does not; the edges are eased.
Both will try to "arrange" accordingly; both understand each other
clearly.

Those who come from countries which operate in this manner
may find business directness hard to accept, until they get used to
the pattern and realize that nothing is meant personally. Their
personal feelings may be hurt from time to time. Though far more
gracious, indirection is a slow approach. Americans look for speed,
for facts, for a clear line. Many others look first for grace, for
kindness, for dignity and other values. The difference is a matter of
priorities.

(See also *Truth or Courtesy?* page 26)

COMPETITION

The predominating goal of business in America is financial profit
which is often referred to here as "the bottom line." It is not family
honor, personal prestige, state revenues, or any of various other
goals that are primary concerns in other cultures. The result is that
this is a highly competitive society; we take it for granted that others
will be the same. Again this relates partly to our time pressure. "The
race is won by the fastest runner," "We must get there first with the
most," are common American sayings. Hence, for example, the
vast sums spent on nationwide advertising campaigns—we compete
for markets from every billboard, newspaper and television screen.
Hurried working lunches at one's desk, quick flights to do business
and return rapidly from far places are part of this time-pressed
competitive pattern. So is the growing number of "workaholics."
These are people so imbued with taking the market, getting to the

top, making a corporate name, that they scarcely take time out for their own families, for recreation or for pleasure.

DECISION MAKING

Contrary to the custom in many countries, decisions are made at various working levels in most American firms. They do not all get made at the top, as is a familiar pattern in many countries. Department (or Division and Section) heads in the U.S.A. frequently consult with those colleagues and subordinates who have relevant knowledge. Then, depending on the type and magnitude of decision being made, they will either make a judgement themselves, or perhaps take the matter to another higher level. Even top executives normally consult one or more individuals, or additional groups—perhaps a Board of Trustees, Directors, or Advisors—if the matter is important, before making their own final—sometimes lonely—decision.

NEGOTIATING

In this country negotiating is done openly and often hard, in negotiating sessions. It is rarely a rubber-stamp confirmation of a decision already made elsewhere, in private discussions. Americans press hard. One can assume that their eye is firmly focussed on the profit potential, whether this be long term or short term. They bargain. Their first figure should be considered negotiable. When they shave a price this should not be read as a sign of uncertainty or lack of trustworthiness, though it may seem so to those whose normal negotiating patterns do not involve bargaining. Compromises are the name of the negotiating game—"I will do this if you will do that."

Putting things down on paper—initial drafts—can seem threatening to people who normally do not put matters on paper until they are firm. Americans, however, find it imperative to get basic essentials down on paper so they can think them over, discuss, revise, and re-evaluate them. No one should feel that a first draft is binding; it is not. *Nothing* is ultimately binding until it is signed by both parties. No one can be held responsible in law until that point, although gentlemen's agreements and shared expressed perceptions are normally honored as the proceedings develop.

Most foreign businessmen who negotiate with Americans will already have had experience along these lines, no doubt. If not, they should discuss American approaches and procedures with a number of people in advance. Negotiating is always a complex process. It is a sensitive area in which cultural differences, priorities and values play a particularly significant role. This fact should be understood from the start.

Chapter 6

Life in the Office

Some office procedures may be unfamiliar.

Again, matters of time and pace crop up. Work days officially start at 9:00 A.M. This should really mean 9 o'clock—not ten past or half past nine. You will find people taking some liberties with starting times, but employers notice this even though they do not necessarily reprimand.

Employees in many nations have a philosophy that one works when the "boss" is present, but any time he is not there, if there is nothing specific or pressing to do, one can relax by reading the newspaper, doing one's fingernails, or otherwise "passing the time" in a personal way. In America one is being paid for one's *time*. Employees are expected to find other work if their own desks are clear, to finish anything pending from previous days, or to help someone else with his work—but never to sit idle. The employer expects value for the money he is spending. He "owns" your time while he is paying for it. The phrase "time is money" means exactly that. The boss is not asking more of you than he is doing himself; he will quite probably work through the lunch hour and even take work home at night.

Employee's lunch hours should be kept within the allotted time (unless one is officially discussing company business). Long lunch-time absences may be overlooked now and then, but not habitually. Also, although others may start getting ready to leave the office a few minutes early, new employees should be careful not to cut the day short. Work until the day officially ends at five o'clock unless you are in an office where "flexi-time" is the accepted procedure. Flexible work hours—starting or ending work earlier or later—is fairly common now in Europe but relatively new in the U.S.A.

Some half-million Americans are now on the system; some people estimate that ten million will have that option by 1985-90. The system is designed to ease traffic and commuting problems, add to family time as more women work, and give people a greater sense of control over their lives. A by-product appears to be greater worker productivity, higher morale, and less absenteeism.

HIRING AND FIRING

Those from lands where family bonds are close are accustomed to family ties being closely meshed with business connections. This rarely happens in America and is generally mistrusted. We call it "nepotism" and fear it as a corrupting influence or the taking of unfair advantage over outsiders. Nor do we develop a "patron" or permanent relationship between employer and employee. In many countries people relax once they have a job, knowing they will almost never be fired (except for a major immorality). Although there are legal protections in America so that employees cannot be unjustly fired without cause, jobs nevertheless are not permanent. Workers must do a good job, produce well, and get along with their colleagues—or they can be "let go" as it is called. This is rarely done without warning, but it is important to be aware of the fact that in the United States one is a member of a business firm and not a family. It makes a difference.

INFORMALITY

The informality found in many offices here can prove to be a difficult adjustment for those who are accustomed to clearly defined "rank" in offices. The protocol of rank often exists here too, especially in large city banks, law firms, or major corporations. But in many establishments the atmosphere is loose and easy with considerable joking, teasing, and wandering in and out of offices among all levels of employees. This may be perplexing at first for a newcomer who does not realize that, despite the informal use of first names and bantering chatter, people really know very well who is the "boss." He does, in fact, hold authority, though outward signs may not be clearly visible.

Informal clothing, such as sweaters, sports jackets or sports shoes, are worn in many offices, especially those outside the large cities. In some areas even blue jeans and/or bright colored shorts, or open-necked shirts, are common. This should not be taken as lack of respect as might be assumed in some countries. Here it has to do with local custom, or weather, but does not relate to respect.

STAFF MEETINGS

Staff meetings are a frequent part of most office routines. Those of all ranks are expected to contribute freely to the discussion if they have something worthwhile to add or suggest. They are not expected to make long speeches nor to speak too many times in the course of a meeting. Make your point briefly and clearly, then be quiet unless asked to develop it more fully. But if you have something worth saying, never hesitate because you feel too inexperienced or too new. People will think you *have* no ideas unless you express them.

COFFEE BREAKS

Nearly all large offices have coffee wagons that circulate for mid-morning and midafternoon coffee "breaks." Although 15 minutes are allotted twice a day for relaxation and chatter, many employees take coffee to their desks and keep on working. In small offices, the coffeepot is often "on" all day and employees take coffee whenever they like or can make tea for themselves.

COLLECTIONS

Don't be startled if someone asks you to make a contribution toward a wedding or retirement present for a fellow employee. This is often done. Everyone contributes a small amount so that a gift can be given in the name of the whole office. You never refuse whether or not you know—or like—the particular recipient. The amount per person is always small, and the requests are infrequent. When you leave, you will have some recognition too!

SOCIAL LIFE

This varies tremendously from office to office. Big corporations may have glee clubs, bowling or baseball teams, trips, dance classes, or other employee activities which you can join or not as you like. Small companies usually do not.

In general people go to lunch with each other by invitation when they so desire; higher rank tends to invite lower rank rather than the other way around, but lines are not closely drawn. Except for special occasions, everyone pays for himself or herself regardless of whether or not an invitation was extended.

It is quite acceptable for men or women colleagues, single or married, to go out together for lunch. This may be the extent to which your office friends will invite you. Although in general Americans readily take people home with them, they often do not want to mix business and social life. If this is the case in your place of work, you will have to seek your friendships through other channels.

If people rush quickly out of the office in the evening without any courtesies, think nothing of it. Often they must travel long distances to get home and are hurrying to catch special trains or buses.

PERQUISITES OR "PERKS"

At the upper staff levels there are some perquisites such as club memberships, cars, and the like; in addition, salesmen take customers fishing or hunting, or to sports events, or theatres sometimes to woo their business. However, "perks" play far less of a role in the U.S.A. than in many countries.

CALLING CARDS

These are widely used in the U.S.A. but not as immediately or universally as they are in some countries. Do with yours whatever is comfortable but do not be surprised if host businessmen in the U.S.A. do not produce them at moments which would seem normal to you. Generally they are exchanged in this country when two people decide they want to be in touch with each other again—not necessarily at the moment of meeting.

Chapter 7

Manners and Courtesies in Social Life

FRIENDSHIPS

In this mobile society of ours, friendships can be close, constant, intense, generous, and real, yet fade away in a short time if circumstances shift. Neither side feels hurt by this. Both may exchange Christmas greetings for a year or two, perhaps a few letters for a while—then no more. If the same two people meet again by chance, even years later, they pick up the friendship where it left off and are delighted. This can be perplexing to those from countries where friendships flower more slowly but then become lifelong attachments, with mutual obligations, extending sometimes deeply into both families.

In the United States you can feel free to visit in people's homes, share their holidays, enjoy their children and their lives without fear that you are taking on a lasting obligation. Do not hesitate to accept hospitality because you cannot reciprocate. No one will expect you to do so for they know you are far from home. Americans will enjoy welcoming you and be pleased if you accept their hospitality easily.

Another perplexity for many people from other countries is that, although Americans include them warmly in their personal everyday lives, they do not demonstrate a high degree of courtesy if it requires a great deal of time. This is the opposite of the practice in some nations where people are unstintingly generous with their time, but do not necessarily admit a guest into the privacy of their home. In some places hosts will appear at airports in the middle of the night to meet even a casual acquaintance; they put their car at the visitor's disposal; they take days off to act as a guide—all evidence of tremendous generosity. But these same people may never introduce their wives or invite the guest to participate in their family life. In both cases the feeling is equally warm; the pattern of expression, however, is different.

Distances, pace, and the pressures of life being what they are in America, together with the fact that without household help, cooking, babysitting, and other domestic responsibilities must be absorbed into each person's day (as well as all professional, community and social demands), Americans extend their welcome warmly at home, but truly cannot manage the time to do a great deal with a visitor outside their daily routine. They will probably expect you to get yourself from the airport to your hotel by public transport; they assume that you will phone them from there; unless you are chairman of the board or a similar dignitary, you may be expected to find your own way (by cab) from the hotel to the host's office (or home).

However, once you arrive there, the welcome will be full and warm and real. Most visitors find themselves readily invited into many homes here. In some countries it is considered inhospitable to entertain at home, offering what is felt as "merely" home-cooked food, not "doing something" for your guest. It is felt that restaurant entertaining shows more respect and welcome. Or for various other reasons, such as crowded space, language difficulties, or family custom, outsiders are not invited into homes.

In the United States both methods are used, but here it is often considered more friendly to invite a person to one's home than to go to a public place, except in purely business relationships. The further one is from big cities, the more likely this becomes. So, if your host or hostess brings you home, do not feel that you are being shown inferior treatment.

· Don't feel neglected if you do not find flowers awaiting you in your hotel room either. This happens graciously in Thailand, the Philippines, the Caribbean, Holland, and many flower-filled lands. But flowers are exceedingly expensive here, hotel delivery is uncertain, arrival times are often delayed, changed, or canceled— so flowers are not customarily sent as a welcoming touch. Please do not feel unwanted! Outward signs vary in different lands; the inward welcome is what matters, and this will be real.

PARTIES

Among the more interesting things to observe as you travel the world are the ways in which people conduct themselves at parties. In some countries men and women drift to opposite ends of the room and talk to one another; in others they sit in large chairs around the edge of the room and talk only to the people on either side of them, or silently eat and observe the scene.

It is normal in some lands for a person to remain patiently silent until he has been introduced, then to talk only to those whom he has "met properly."

As you would imagine, Americans move about a great deal at parties. At small gatherings they may sit down, but as soon as there are more people than chairs in a room—or better yet, a little before this point—you will see first one and then another make some excuse to get to his feet (to fetch a drink or greet a friend or open a window) until soon everyone is standing, moving around, chatting with one group and then another. Sitting becomes static beyond a certain point. We expect people to move about and be "self-starters." It is quite normal for Americans to introduce themselves; they will drift around a room stopping to talk wherever they like, introducing themselves and their companions. If this happens, you are expected to reply by giving your name and introducing the person with you; then at least the men generally shake hands. Sometimes the women do so as well, but often they merely nod and smile. A man usually shakes a woman's hand only if she extends it. Otherwise he too just nods and greets her.

After such an informal introduction, you talk together for a little while (here come those questions): "Are you new here?" "How long have you been in America?" "Did you bring your children with you?" Within a moment or two, you will have struck some common ground, conversation will move along for a while, and then *either* couple can feel free to say something informal like: "Well, it's been nice to meet you" or "I hope we see you again soon." This is the signal for both couples to say their "adieus" and drift off to another group.

The basic rule at big parties is: *don't stay in one place for too long.* Pick out people you think look interesting, then go talk to them. Women should not cluster in a group with each other or hide themselves away in a corner. They too move around the room either with their husbands or escort or alone, whichever they prefer, unless they are strategically located (and attractive!) so that people keep coming up to them. The point of a party in this country is to meet and talk with people; the fact that you are all there together under your host's roof is in itself a form of introduction in our view. As a result, anyone can feel free to talk to anyone else.

When you first arrive at a large party, the host or hostess may introduce you to two or three people nearby, but if others are still arriving, he or she may then return to greet newcomers, expecting you to go on by yourself, moving from group to group. If this feels too uncomfortable and frightening, it is quite all right to say to someone: "I am a stranger here and know no one. Could you introduce me to some of the people?" Almost anyone will feel flattered that you turned to him for help and will gladly take you under his wing, introducing you and easing your discomfort.

Our easy-come-and-go pattern is unfamiliar to people from many other countries. Like much else about the nation, it stems in large measure from our size, our numbers, and our constantly shifting population.

INVITATIONS

Written

One should answer any written invitation as soon as possible. Some will have R.S.V.P. or "please reply" written at the bottom. Such invitations *require* an answer, but even if such a request is not included, it is still a courtesy to let the host know whether (or not) you expect to attend. If a telephone number is given, you can phone; otherwise it is best to write a small note, either accepting or regretting.

By Telephone

When accepting an invitation over the telephone, make it a habit always to repeat four things: 1) the day of the week, 2) the date, 3) the time, and 4) the place. Then you are *sure* you have understood it correctly. If you do not know how to get to the host's home, this is the moment to ask for directions and to *write them down*.

Since telephones are so widespread that communication is easy in the United States, it is considered thoughtless and rude to accept an invitation and then not appear without phoning your regrets *in advance*. If something prevents you from attending, you *always* telephone your host or hostess immediately, just as soon as you know you will not be able to go. Explain the circumstances and express your apologies. Do it *before* the party, as far ahead of time as you can. The host may want to invite someone else in your place or, if you are the guest of honor, may change the date of the party to suit your schedule.

Impersonal

Much social life in this country takes place at communal parties of one kind or another—group activities sponsored by a church, a school, a company division, or a club. These may be dinners, picnics, tours, weekend camping or skiing trips, lectures, concerts, receptions, bowling evenings, or any of a wide variety of affairs. If you have some connection with the sponsoring group, you can assume that you will be welcome to join in any such gathering. Many others are open to you whether or not you have a connection. If you see a poster announcing an event, or read a notice, or find a note in the newspaper, don't wait to be invited. Just go if you can, knowing that no one else will receive a personal invitation either. Such community affairs are friendly and an excellent way to meet new neighbors. If in doubt as to whether or not you would be welcome, just ask someone. But do not feel hesitant just because you were not specifically invited. If it is a cooperative party, do your share of the work and cooperate in the fun too!

WHEN TO ARRIVE AND LEAVE

For meals:

You should arrive at the time indicated in the invitation or within five to seven minutes of that time. If you are very early, walk around the block or wait in your car or downstairs in the lobby. In this country the hostess is also likely to be the cook. Give her those precious last moments in peace to compose her soul; don't arrive *before* the time you were asked for. If you find you are going to be late, it is a real help to your hostess if you telephone and tell her so. She may turn off the stove and be grateful to you for not having spoiled supper by your lateness.

Cocktail parties, receptions, teas:

Invitations for such events usually say "from X hour to Y hour"— 5:00 to 7:00 P.M., for example. This means that you can come any time that suits you between those hours. You do not have to leave on the dot of the time indicated, but should go within a half hour at the latest.

For a dance:

It is usual to arrive half an hour to an hour after it starts. There is nothing more dreary than a dance that has not yet gotten under way, unless you are a true dancer who likes the floor uncrowded and the orchestra fresh!

For the theater:

Plan to arrive at least ten minutes before curtain time. You will want to take off your coat, read the program, and settle down before the play begins.

Weddings, funerals, public lectures, sports events:

Be there about ten minutes *before* the specified time so that you will be seated and relaxed by the time it starts.

Business appointments:

Arrive exactly at the moment of appointment or a few minutes *ahead.* It is considered a discourtesy to keep a busy person waiting. If he keeps you waiting, however, take it in good grace. The person whose office is the scene of the meeting takes precedence. If you do not want to give him this advantage, arrange to meet in your office or on some "neutral" ground such as at a club or in a hotel lobby.

DRINKING

Drinking habits vary widely among Americans. Some families never serve any alcoholic beverages. Others have cocktails before dinner, wine with the meal, and/or after-dinner drinks. You are more likely to be offered a cocktail before dinner than to be served wine with the meal. If you are not accustomed to American cocktails, be cautious; they are often quite strong. Ladies as well as men drink them, but you should not feel any hesitation in asking for a sherry, Dubonnet, or nonalcoholic drink (such as Coca-Cola or fruit juice) if you do not want a cocktail. In some homes the cocktail hour may become quite lengthy. If it does and you do not wish to drink additional cocktails, it is perfectly all right to refuse. You can also drink as slowly as you like. It is a good idea to eat some of the food which is offered with drinks; there are usually cheese and crackers, olives, peanuts, potato chips with creamy "dips" or other small snacks.

If the host asks: "What will you have to drink?" you can reply: "What are the possibilities?" or you may request a particular drink as you prefer.

Common cocktails offered in most homes include:

Gin and tonic:

A particularly popular summer drink made with gin, quinine water, and ice—often with a sprig of mint and slice of lemon or lime.

Scotch or bourbon:

Either type of whiskey is served with water or with soda or "on the rocks." This last phrase means simply that liquor is poured over ice with nothing added. You can ask for "on the rocks with a little water" if you want it somewhat less strong.

Martini:

Colorless but powerful; a short drink made with dry vermouth and gin.

Manhattan:

Sweet and dark colored, made with sweet vermouth and whiskey.

Bloody Mary:

A mild drink, often offered before lunch, made of spiced tomato juice with a "shot" (an ounce) of vodka or gin.

You can have your drinks "straight up"(without ice) or with ice. Iced drinks are not quite so strong, especially after the ice has melted a bit. Americans use more ice than almost anyone else in the world. They also have their drinks "short" or "tall," meaning with or without soda (or water) to fill a tall glass.

When men stop for a drink together on their way home, the one who made the suggestion often pays for the first drink; the companion frequently offers to pay for a second. This is no hard-and-fast rule—they may each pay for their own. Normally if no one extended an invitation but a group of men just find themselves at a bar together, each pays his own bill. Mar. businessmen have a drink over a business lunch. If you do not want to do this, have no hesitation about declining; it is not a "must." Beer is also often taken at lunch.

Wine is being drunk increasingly in the United States, but it still is
not found as commonly as in many other countries. Do not be surprised if you are offered milk, coffee, tea (iced or hot depending on
the season), or even Coca-Cola with a meal. Water is not always
served, but feel free to .sk for it if you want it, either in a home or a
restaurant.

WHEN INVITED BY A FAMILY

This is likely to be informal and relaxed. You will probably be
served "family style." Platters will be passed from person to person
or the host (or hostess) may serve from one end of the table. All ages
eat together. The wife who, in this servantless country, has usually
prepared the meal often does not wait on table as is customary in
many countries. A common family division of labor is for the wife
to prepare the meal, the husband to handle the cocktail hour, and
the young people or husband, rather than the wife, to change the
plates between courses.

Whether or not you help with the dishes afterward will vary depending on your rank and age, how often you have been to the
home, and family custom. Many families do not permit guests to do
any work on the first visit, but if they become frequent guests in the
house, then they gradually join in with the various household chores
as these occur. Some people *never* let a guest help; it is a good idea to
offer, but then take your cue from the response.

Men do a good deal more around an American house than is true
in many parts of the world. There is growing flexibility about this;
either sex does whatever needs doing in many households-
—including even caring for the baby. Usually men at least take out
the trash and help wash dishes. Men usually cut the grass and take
care of major outdoor jobs; women look after the flower gardens
and do much "ferrying" in the family car, especially if there are a
number of children, all needing to be taken and fetched from
school, sports, dentists, birthday parties, and the like.

At meals, it is the custom to wait for the hostess to begin eating and to finish as closely as you can to when everyone else does. Watch your hostess from time to time to judge your own speed. Americans tend to eat rather more quickly than many other people; you may be embarrassed if you find yourself far behind everyone else at the end of the meal.

If for religious (or other) reasons there are some foods you cannot eat, just leave them quietly without calling attention to the fact if possible; otherwise explain in advance to your hostess. Even though at first American food may be different and you may not enjoy it, it will please your hostess if you eat at least some of every dish and express appreciation for her efforts. She will probably have extended herself in trying to please you.

The American habit of shifting the fork from right to left hand when the knife is used—then back again—is unfamiliar to many. Don't feel you must struggle with that system. Either method is perfectly acceptable, so do whatever is comfortable for you. It is *not* considered correct to soak up gravy with bread, to tuck your napkin under your chin, or to make any kind of slurping, burping, or other noises while eating or at the table.

BUFFET MEALS

Buffet meals—called "fork suppers" in England—are a popular means of entertaining because they are informal and easy to handle even without household help. There are no exact rules about what is proper; your hostess will indicate how she wants people to proceed and where they are to sit. You can probably tell just by watching other guests. Systems vary from household to household depending on the way the house is arranged, whether the garden is being used, how many people there are, and so on. Often folding snack tables are provided; if you find it difficult to balance your plate or cut your meat, don't hesitate to seek out the corner of a more solid table and pull your chair up to it so that you are comfortable. Nobody will mind. The point is for people to feel at ease and to have a pleasant, relaxed time together.

You will naturally thank a hostess as you leave, but if you want to be considered really polite and pleasant drop her a note within a day or two after the event. This will be greatly appreciated. If you prefer, you can express your thanks by telephone instead. This should be done on the day immediately following the party. Not everyone does this, but it is not difficult and gives a nice warm feeling that lasts a long time with your host family.

BRINGING GIFTS

Although it is always welcome and gracious, it is not necessary in this country, as it is in some others, to bring flowers or a gift when you are invited for lunch or dinner, except on special occasions such as a birthday or Christmas. If you have visited several times before, you may want to bring an occasional small "thank you" token of appreciation, but generally speaking it is a highly optional matter. We go in and out of each other's houses so informally and so often that gifts are by no means expected. If you do bring something, it should be small and simple—a "gesture" rather than a gift— perhaps a tiny souvenir of your country or a single rose or a small trinket or a jar of honey or something equally modest.

If you are going to be an *overnight* or *weekend* guest, however, it is customary to bring the hostess a small present—often an appropriate book, a box of candy, a bottle of wine, a small bottle of perfume, or some similar gift.

PRECEDENCE OF MEN AND WOMEN

Who goes first and who follows, and the extent to which women are "emancipated" are some of the remaining variables in today's social world. Women in the United States are reasonably accepted in the business world and even more so in society, in educational establishments, and in community endeavors. They take part in sports activities with their husbands and often travel widely with them, even on business trips. However, despite their growing sense of equality, most of them still expect, receive, and cherish a number of small special courtesies.

Many men still rise when ladies enter the room on a social occasion—rarely in business—although the custom is fading with the younger generation and under the impact of Women's Lib. Nonetheless, most women (of all ages) still appreciate this courtesy when it occurs!

Men usually open doors for ladies, but then they stand back and allow them to go through first—different from Korea, for example, where women traditionally follow. The exception here may sometimes be for a revolving door; since this is heavy, men normally go first to push for the ladies.

Women in the United States walk *ahead* of men into a room or theater or restaurant unless there is business to be done—such as choosing a table, handling tickets, buying a program. Then the man goes ahead to attend to the details. Women precede men into theater rows or church pews—different from Germany, for example.

In a sense American women have the best of both worlds, both independence and special attention. Some American women can be overwhelming to women whose pattern is more retiring. American ebullience, drive, and energy can seem frightening; they are not meant to be. Some women do appear noisy, aggressive, dominating, but you will find many others who are quiet, content, gentle. The only thing to do is to take each one as she is and make no generalizations until you have observed the women here for several months.

UNESCORTED WOMEN

Women who are alone are far more free here than in many parts of the world; one sees many unescorted women. But, unfortunately, this is a time of great turmoil in the United States. Crime is widespread, and certain precautions are necessary. Except perhaps for hijacking, you can feel safe in airplanes, buses, or trains day or night, but most terminals are best avoided after midnight.

It is safe for a woman to drive long distances alone in her own car if she wants to do so. Service station men and hotel (or motel) clerks will give friendly help; if there is trouble with the car along the way, a single woman will nearly always get help from passersby or high-way patrolmen. But if a woman is driving alone in a city, it is wiser for her to keep the doors of her car locked and her purse out of sight. These two simple habits can prevent someone from jumping quickly into the car at a stop light or grabbing the purse through an open window.

Cities have become less safe after dark, mostly, alas, because an in-creasing number of people are doing desperate things in search of money for a "fix"—the price of the day's drug. The drug or alcohol problem in the United States is acute. Stay on well-populated and well-lit streets; do not walk in parks at night; take taxis after about 9:00 P.M. Do hold your purse carefully and don't let shoulder purses hang loosely. Don't wear gold necklaces or bracelets visibly. With the high price of gold, they may be snatched from you in many cities.

It is best to ask locally which streets are—and which are not—safe. Looks can be deceiving. . .dark and poor-looking areas can be safe; well-lit ones may be dangerous at quiet times (like Wall Street after the business world goes home).

A woman can go alone into a restaurant for either lunch or din-ner, though usually avoids sophisticated, expensive restaurants in big cities or fancy night clubs with floor shows and/or dancing. Single women usually avoid public bars unless they want to go to one of those open expressly for singles. They can go comfortably to cocktail lounges in hotels or good restaurants.

Etiquette varies somewhat across the country as to whether or not a lone woman talks to people at neighboring tables or in adjoining seats. Let your own intuition be your guide. It depends on the ap-pearance of your neighbor and your own personality. Broadly speaking, people get friendlier and more casual as you go further and further west in the U.S.; they tend to be more outgoing in small towns than in large cities. In today's world it is generally advisable for a single woman not to hold a sustained conversation with a single man who approaches her in any public place in one of the large cities. A few words and a smile are fine, but if a man pursues a conversation he may well be on the search for a "pickup." Avoid letting him see or overhear your address or room number.

Single women are of course frequently asked to cocktail parties, buffet suppers, picnics, or outings of various kinds. There is no reason why they cannot accept and also return such invitations, inviting single men to their apartments for dinner, or a party, either alone or in a group. Women do not offer to pay for meals, taxis, and the like if they have been invited out, but do expect to pay their own way if they go out on business meetings, lunches, or appointments. However, if a man offers to pick up such bills, one accepts graciously. He will probably put it on his expense account anyway!

ADULT DATING

Men and women go out together a great deal, especially in the cities of America; they ski together, work together, dine together, either at restaurants or in each other's apartments. This does not mean that they are necessarily interested in having sex together, though it may appear so and, of course, with some men and women it is so.

To an Arab, an African, or a Latin, or to many of the other men of the world, the fact that a girl will so readily go off alone with him often seems to imply that she is sexually available. This is not true. It is important to realize this from the start. You will scare off many American girls if you rush in too fast; they may seem very friendly, yet have no intention whatsoever of having sex with you at the first meeting or, for that matter, at any other time. Most American women are not promiscuous.

If you have a wife at home, be sure to let this fact be known to the woman early in your acquaintance. It will not necessarily make any difference, but the woman wants to know the situation. She will feel tricked and frequently will drop the man immediately if she thinks he has cheated, lied, or otherwise misled her.

Single men dating American women should have more than one date with them before making any move to develop the situation into something more intimate. In today's world of free speech, you can ask a woman how she feels about "going further." But your chances will be poor if you move too fast too soon, regardless of how informal things may look here.

A woman will not feel that she owes you sex because you have paid for her dinner. She will feel that her company and her acceptance of you have contributed toward a pleasant evening for both, but not that she owes you more. You have to win anything beyond a casual friendship by being the kind of person she likes and wants. You cannot buy this by offering her a meal or material inducements, as though she were a prostitute.

American women are accustomed to easy companionability and equality. With the current emphasis on Women's Lib, many are especially touchy about their independence. The bully approach never did work well here; nowadays it is completely out. Some men feel that women like to be dominated; they boast about how they can "handle" women and feel they can "order," "demand," or "compel" and "have women eating out of their hand." Anyone who comes here expecting to find American women meek, obedient, or submissive is likely to have a hard time.

Paying for Dates

A general rule of thumb is that a woman in business or college will pay her own way during the day. If, however, a man asks her to something special outside normal working hours—for cocktails or dinner or a dance or the movies—the invitation itself means "come

as my guest.'' If a man wants to accompany her but does not want to
pay the bill, he asks differently, thereby letting her know in advance.
He will say ''Are you planning to go to the football game? If so,
shall we sit together?'' or ''I was thinking of going to the theater if I
can get tickets. Would you be interested? If so, what price range
would suit you?''

The growing sense of male-female equality often includes financial equality too, particularly with young people. Women find it
perfectly normal to pay their way especially if, as is often the case,
they are earning the same salary as the man.

The whole matter of ''dating'' is in transition. Young men and
women are quite open and candid in talking over who will pay and
for what. You, too, can feel quite free to ask your friends what the
situation is wherever you are.

Women from Abroad

Single women coming to a job in the United States will often have
to work a bit at finding ways to meet men. Men in offices are likely
to be family men who rush out at five o'clock to catch a commuter
train back home to wife and children; office bachelors often turn
out to be wary of dating someone they will see every day. Many fear
developing a closer relationship than they want with an office
colleague.

The best way for a single woman to meet men or other women easily is likely to be through sports activities or some kind of club. Go
skiing or join a bowling team; play golf or tennis; take a membership in a swimming club. If you are not athletic, enroll in an evening
class that appeals to both sexes—choosing photography, ballroom
dancing, judo, or computer programming for instance, rather than
fashion design, or piano, or pottery. Select your hobby with a little
thought!

If you are asked for a date, remember that you can set the pace. In
this country the man generally does the inviting and the planning,
but he is likely to find out first what will please his guest. You
probably will have an opportunity to indicate the kinds of

things you enjoy: mountain climbing or listening to music; being with a group or eating alone together by candlelight. In addition to choosing along such lines, it is you who also set the level of friendship. You can keep things platonic if you want to. If the man seems increasingly affectionate and you want it to be otherwise, you can make that clear. The woman has the choice.

Most big cities contain numerous young men and women who come from elsewhere to work and find it hard to meet new people. Many places therefore have developed what are known as "Singles Clubs." These can be free-for-all marriage markets; they should be avoided. They can also, however, be extremely nice clubs, offering excellent sports facilities, good theater parties, cocktail parties, and the like to help newcomers become acquainted. They usually publish a monthly booklet or have a bulletin board describing the range of activities that will take place that month. If interested, you go to whichever parties or events you choose. If you find congenial people of either sex, that is fine. If not, you drift on home and try again on some other occasion. There are always people at the door to introduce you and make it easy for you to meet and mix, even if you are alone.

Start easily if you join such a group. Be a little cool at first. The super-friendly type who rushes to make friends may in fact be the club bore looking for a new audience. Give yourself time to look over the situation before you become too friendly with anyone. Clubs of this sort are often found through church contacts; otherwise ask around, or watch the local newspapers.

FINDING "FACILITIES"

A newly arrived Scot was asked what had been the most difficult thing for him on his first day in the United States. Without a moment's hesitation, he answered: "Finding a Men's Room."

Some countries have public conveniences plainly visible on the street or small buildings that are clearly marked. The United States does not. Americans find their way to facilities in such public places as gasoline stations, which are usually clean. There is no charge though one may have to ask the attendant for a key because they are kept locked. Also try restaurants, libraries, museums, department stores, airports. Bus terminal or railroad station toilets are apt to be unpleasant, but can be found. *Never* use the rest rooms in subways.

You can always go into a hotel and use the facilities whether or not you are registered there as a guest; you will usually find them somewhere off the main lobby.

Don't be confused by the name on the door. Sometimes it is marked "Men" or "Women" or "Ladies" or "Dames". Often the term is "Rest Rooms." Especially in restaurants, there may be no word used at all but a picture of an old-fashioned girl or a rooster or some other clue may be painted on the door. Women's rooms are often delicately called "Powder Rooms." The European terms "Comfort Station" or "W.C." are rarely used but generally understood.

If you are in need, just ask for the "Men's Room" or "Ladies' Room."

In a large hotel or restaurant, leave a tip in the small saucer if there is an attendant—25¢ is common. One does *not* tip in clubs, but a smile and a friendly word are appreciated.

as gasoline stations, which are usually clean. There is no charge though one may have to ask the attendant for a key because they are kept locked. Also try restaurants, libraries, museums, department stores, airports. Bus terminal or railroad station toilets are apt to be unpleasant, but can be found. Never use the rest rooms in subways. You can always go into a hotel and use the facilities whether or not you are registered there as a guest; you will usually find them somewhere off the main lobby.

Don't be confused by the name on the door. Sometimes it is marked "Men" or "Women" or "Ladies" or "Dames". Often the term is "Rest Rooms." Especially in restaurants, there may be no word used at all but a picture of an old-fashioned girl or a rooster or some other clue may be painted on the door. Women's rooms are often delicately called "Powder Rooms." The European terms "Comfort Station" or "W.C." are rarely used but generally understood.

If you are in need, just ask for the "Men's Room" or "Ladies' Room."

In a large hotel or restaurant, leave a tip in the small saucer if there is an attendant—25¢ is common. One does not tip in clubs, but a smile and a friendly word are appreciated.

Practical Pointers

Chapter 8

Clothes

Winter temperatures throughout much of the country range from 0 °F (or below) to more or less 50 °F (—20 ℃ to 10 ℃). One should be prepared for a good deal of wind. Fur or leather coats or coats with quilted or furlike linings are needed in many places in the north because of the wind. There is often snow, but in most cities it is quickly cleared, especially in the northernmost part of the country.

Indoors, in winter, buildings are likely to be kept somewhere between 60°-68°. You will need lightweight wool for winter with additional sweaters, jackets, stoles, ponchos, or the like to put on or take off easily as you move from hot to cold, from air conditioning to heat, from outdoors to indoors. Those who come from hot climates will perhaps feel drafts quite readily at first, especially in country houses, and should be prepared with layers, such as extra scarves or sweaters, and warm underwear.

For much of the country and much of the year, you will need heavy *outdoor* clothing, including boots, overcoat, warm gloves, and hat. You can buy these garments here at reasonable prices. You will need a raincoat—the combination kind with removable zip-out lining is especially useful—to be worn during the four inbetween months of spring and autumn (April-May and September-October).

Most boys in the United States wear long trousers (rather than shorts, which are worn primarily for sports occasions) from the time they are about six years old—often earlier. People in general like bright colors and patterns; dress is informal, even in the cities. Few women wear hats, for example, except for wind and cold or for really dressy occasions such as weddings. Dark business suits for men and short cocktail dresses or dressy pantsuits for women suffice at most evening functions. People rarely "dress" (wear tuxedoes and long evening dresses) for the theater except on Opening Nights. If "dress" is required at someone's home, you will be told "Black Tie." This, too, is rare, even in key cities.

Children dress very casually. They usually wear simple, "drip-dry" or "perma-prest"play clothes except for special occasions when they are dressed in "party clothes." In some parochial schools and a small number of private schools, uniforms are required, but this is unusual. Boys and girls generally wear a variety of sturdy and simple clothes to school, often jeans or corduroy slacks. A few schools still require jackets and ties, for boys, but the trend for young people is increasingly individualistic—even bizarre. Dress-up occasions can be quite competitive, ranging anywhere from "doing your own thing" to ruffles and frills and starched collars, depending primarily on the geography. Speaking broadly, the South and Midwest tend to be more conventional than either coast.

Chapter 9

Moving Around Your New City

You get yourself around a city on foot or by bus, taxi, your own car, or (in some cities) by subway...just as you do anywhere else in cities.

ON FOOT

If distances are short or you need to go in two directions (east *and* west or north *and* south), the quickest way to go may be on foot. Our needs are supplied in large measure by huge trucks and vans that converge on each town or city in the early morning, disgorge, and move out again. During working hours, in many cities, when these vehicles are unloading their massive piles of foodstuffs, clothes, raw materials, and other goods, street traffic can become so congested that it almost stops. Union regulations and the cost of overtime pay prevent such unloading being done at night, except under special circumstances. So people often get to their destination most quickly on foot if distances permit.

BY BUS

Trams or trolley cars are now obsolete in most United States cities; generally the public travels by bus. More and more cities are requiring passengers to have the exact change in hand as they board the bus—or else "tokens" (small coinlike pieces similar to the French "jeton") that can be bought in advance. Labor here is so expensive that conductors were long ago taken off our buses. For some years drivers had the double job of making change at the same time that they were operating their monster buses through traffic. This relatively new "exact change" rule eases the driver load; it speeds service for everyone; it also reduces the number of robberies that were taking place when drivers had a great deal of extra money for making change.

In many cities bus and subway tokens can be used interchangeably, and are bought at subway booths. It is a great timesaver to buy tokens in considerable quantity and keep them in a special purse or envelope so that you can get at them easily. Otherwise you may have to wait in long lines in rush hour or get caught without change just when you need to catch a bus.

School children and people over sixty-five years of age can get special passes in most cities so that they can ride at reduced rates during certain hours of the day.

BY TAXI

Because at first they feel uncertain, most people are likely to travel by taxi when they arrive in any new place. Here taxis definitely come under the heading of luxury travel. In Chicago, for example, the meter reads almost $1.00 before you even move! Furthermore, taxis have an aggravating way of being hard to find not only at the busy hours of a day but also if the weather turns bad.

In some cities you can telephone to call them (see local phone book for numbers) but in others, including New York, you hail them on the street or find them at a hack stand.

Generally speaking, taxis are metered throughout the country, but there are some cities (for example, Washington, D.C.) where they operate on a distance zone system.

If you find yourself sharing a cab with several strangers (legal in some cities but not in others), you will often be expected to pay full price, unfair though that may seem. Nothing is uniform in the U.S. You will need to ask your fellow riders or the driver about the rules; they vary from city to city.

Although drivers do not always comply, the regulations are: they must stop if not showing an off-duty sign; they must drive anywhere within the city limits; they may not ask your destination before you get in and then refuse to take you; they may not charge more than is registered on the meter except for trunks, and bridge, tunnel, or ferry tolls.

There are various sizes of cabs. Often they are not permitted to carry more than four people—sometimes as few as three. Some can carry five or six passengers.

In heavily congested areas the driver may not be allowed by law to get out of his cab to open doors or help with luggage. Do not assume he is being discourteous—it may be a safety measure.

If you want to make a complaint about taxi service, note the driver's number and name (posted somewhere inside the cab). Be sure to get the *name of the taxi company* also—there are many companies in all cities. When you write to the company, be sure to keep a copy of your letter.

BY SUBWAY

Subways are by far the quickest way to move about. Networks of them lie under a number of cities, operating day and night. Most of the time they are filled with people and can be used safely. There are a few warnings, however, that should be observed:

1) Naturally you avoid rush hours if you can. Subways are crammed from about 8:00 to 9:30 A.M. and again from about 4:30 to 6:00 or 6:30 P.M. (These are naturally the hours when pickpockets do their best work, too.)

2) Choose to sit in cars where there are other people rather than empty ones.

3) For safety while waiting for a train, stand near the token booth.

4) Hold your purse firmly and consciously—don't let it dangle. Men should carry wallets in inside not hip pockets. If carrying real valuables (passport, money roll, etc.) safety pin your inside jacket pocket.

5) Save yourself trouble by buying tokens in quantity if you plan to use subways regularly.

YOUR OWN CAR

Costs

Owning a car in any U.S. city is expensive. In addition to the original cost of the car, one has to pay heavy insurance premiums. Rates vary by city and by coverage, but one can pay well over $1,000.00 each year in insurance alone in congested cities.

In addition, the car must be registered and licensed (fee depends on the weight of the car, but ranges from $15 to $60 or more). The cost of a driver's license must be added to that. The high cost of gasoline hardly needs comment.

There are no Customs or other duty charges on a private imported car if it is shipped home again within one year; however, if you sell it in the United States within a year, you will have to pay duty—3 percent of the appraised value of the car at the time of import (as of this writing). Be *sure* to bring your registration papers or proof of ownership. This is very important. Check with your nearest U.S. Consulate on latest rulings and charges before you come, or else with your local automobile club. There are also strict regulations regarding the pollution emissions of cars.

Licensing

If you bring your car, it is recommended that you get an international registration marker for it before leaving home. You will be allowed to drive to your destination with your national license plates or tags, but immediately on arrival you must obtain American license plates from the state in which you will be living. Each state has its own Department of Motor Vehicles (see telephone directory for address) which issues forms for both license and registration. Motorists will have to take a test and secure a U.S. driver's license unless they come from a country which is party to the International Convention on Road Traffic (1949) or the Inter-American Convention (1943), in which case they must carry an international driving permit.

Age minimum for the driver's license varies somewhat by state in the United States, but generally it is sixteen years of age or over. Driver training courses are required in some states. It is wise to have at least a few hours of professional instruction *no matter how well you drive* to learn rules of the road, local requirements, and especially American "driving psychology". This varies considerably from country to country—a Brazilian, Greek, Japanese, and Briton are all different behind a wheel; so are Americans.

Each state Motor Vehicle Bureau will give you a free booklet on request covering local rules. It is important to remember; *ignorance of the law is never considered an excuse* if you run into trouble. You are expected to learn the law and abide by it when you drive.

Automobile Insurance

It is imperative to protect yourself adequately with liability insurance (covering damage to the other person). A few states have not yet made it compulsory, but you should insure yourself at a good substantial level, not the minimum. If you should hit anyone, damages charged here can be astronomically high. Lawyers assume that insurance companies (not the individual) will pay, so they ask damage fees accordingly. If you are *not* covered, you can be financially ruined by gigantic fees charged for injury, fright, shock, or other complaints—even if the accident appeared to you to be slight. Not everyone presses such suits, but enough people do so that you need to be well protected.

Buying a Car

Barring any strikes or emergency delays, you receive delivery on a new car quite quickly in this country. American manufacturers are still building cars with a great deal of horsepower and low mileage per gallon of gas. Since the gasoline crises of the 1970's however, more small, fuel-efficient cars are being built in the U.S. Small foreign cars (especially from Germany and Japan) are also very popular, and, in general, foreign cars are easy to obtain and keep repaired.

Don't buy a car at what is called "List Price" until you have talked to a number of people about it. Prices can usually be bargained down and can vary considerably. Prices also vary markedly from one month to another depending on how near the time is to the appearance of new models. Sometimes dealers then try to get rid of last year's model, and one can get a good bargain as a result. Ask and explore; don't buy too fast.

Car dealers make their greatest profit in two ways: 1) on extras and 2) on arranging the financing and insurance. Let us look at both of these points:

Extras. These are the multitude of "optional" features which all dealers try hard to sell: radios, cassette players, special paint color, air conditioning, fancy seat covers, other items that are not "standard." Dealers are skilled at selling these items, but *you do not need to buy them.* If you are persuaded by a clever talker, it may cost you a considerable amount of extra money.

Financing and Insuring. Dealers normally charge higher interest rates than banks when they arrange the terms of financing. Over the months or years of payment, this can mount up to a considerable amount. Look into alternative possibilities *before* you go to buy. Generally, you will do better to take out your own bank loan rather than work through a car dealer—after all, he must take his share and then he too, will be working with a bank. He will do his best to persuade you to finance the car through him, but it is not required. Don't feel obligated.

Secondhand Cars

The drop in value of American cars after a year or two is so great that many people buy used cars rather than new ones. Prices depend on the age of the car, its condition, its size and make, the locality of the country where it is bought, and the time of year.

Rule #1: in buying a secondhand car, don't even consider buying one that is older than four years;

Rule #2: never go alone. Take someone with you who not only knows cars well, but also knows the ways of American dealers.

Often it is an advantage to go to an area where wealthy people live to find your car. They turn their cars in more often than poor people and the cars are normally in better condition.

Used-car dealers vary widely as to reliability; try to deal with one that has been recommended as reliable. Generally speaking, your chances will be better with a reputable dealer than at a used car lot though you will see these in profusion outside most big cities.

Many people do their buying outside city limits for several reasons: 1) the dealer's reputation is more vulnerable in a small environment so he tends to be more careful than in the anonymity of a large city; 2) one can avoid paying city sales taxes. In New York City, for example, there is a 8 percent sales tax on the price of any purchase. If you can avoid this by going outside the city your saving will be considerable.

It takes time and trouble to buy a secondhand car. If you do not have a friend or colleague who knows cars well, take a garage mechanic with you. It would be worth what you have to pay him for his time. Many mechanics are glad to do such "consulting" work after hours or on weekends. Determine the price of this service in advance, however.

Be sure you actually *drive* the car before buying. You will be allowed to try it. Take it immediately to a nearby garage and ask the mechanic to test it out and give you an opinion as to its condition. There are certain key parts that will give him a quick idea of the car's general condition. It is worth paying something for a careful going-over by a mechanic whom you trust. Do this *before* you sign any papers. Before you buy any car—new or used—talk to people at your office or any friends you have made. There are various tricks of the trade that you should know.

Renting a Car

With street parking so difficult, parking rates so high, and streets so crowded, increasing numbers of city dwellers find owning a car in the city frustrating. Instead, they are using public transportation for everyday use and renting cars only when they need them for out-of-town trips or vacations. Most overseas visitors are likely to find this by far the cheapest and easiest method too. There are many rental companies everywhere. One can rent by the day, week, month, or year.

Your own firm may have a special discount arrangement with a particular rental agency—companies often do. It is worth asking about this at work. Some agencies have had bad experiences and will not rent to people from abroad because of past insurance difficulties or problems with payments. On the other hand, other agencies give additional discounts to vistors from abroad as a special courtesy. You will need to explore a bit and make inquiries, for it all depends on what their experience has been.

Costs are usually determined by time-plus-mileage charges, with insurance and maintenance included in the basic rental cost. However, there are other options: some agencies include the gasoline, others do not; some require that you return the car to its starting point, others will rent cars for one-way travel between cities.

Theft of Cars and from Cars

Unfortunately, the stealing of cars is quite common. You can expect little sympathy if your car was not locked or if the key was left in the ignition—even if the car *was* locked. The registration papers and your driver's license should be kept with you and not in the glove compartment where they would be convenient for the thief but not for you in trying to recover a stolen car! If you want to keep these papers in the car, be *sure* to keep photocopies in a safe place at home as well.

Care should be taken regarding any possessions left in the car. If you must leave something, put it in the trunk or out of sight on the floor even if the car is locked. If traveling across the country in a loaded car, try to park it where you can see it when you stop for meals. At night take all visible items with you into your motel or hotel. Put the rest in the locked trunk. Again this thievery is a part of the turmoil of our times.

Gasoline and Service Stations

Prices vary by state depending on local taxes. The cheapest variety of gasoline, called "Regular," is perfectly good except for high-powered engines, high altitudes, or cars requiring "unleaded" gas.

The U.S. gallon is slightly smaller than the British "imperial gallon," approximately four liters according to the metric system.

One can order by asking for a specific number of gallons or by price ("$8 worth please") or just asking to have the tank "filled up." Most tanks hold 10 to 20 gallons when full.

Routine free services which one can expect (or ask for) at service stations include: checking the oil, tires, and water in the battery; cleaning the windshield; use of their rest rooms (gas stations are the normal places to stop when on a long trip). One does not tip gas station attendants for any of these services. Many stations have "self-service" pumps where motorists put in their own gas at a slightly reduced price—and forego other services (although anyone can use the Rest Rooms).

If your engine is hot, the attendant should not be asked to check the water in your radiator and may decline to do so. So many attendants have been badly burned by gushing steam that this is no longer a regular service—as it used to be.

Traffic Rules

Cars travel on the right throughout the United States. One must by law signal not only for all turns but also for changes of lane. Traffic laws are being enforced more and more strictly as congestion problems grow ever more acute in American cities. Police may travel in unmarked cars; speed regulations are often checked by radar.

If you hear the sirens of fire trucks, ambulances, or police cars approaching, *immediately* pull over to the right and stop or slow down to let them pass.

Horn blowing is not allowed in most cities; don't try to move traffic along by using your horn. You could be fined.

If you come to a yellow school bus at a standstill—even if it has stopped on the opposite side of the road—*stop your car*. This law is strictly enforced because children may be running across the road to or from the bus.

Never stop your car on a highway. If you have a problem or want to read a map or change drivers, drive it (or push it) well to the side of the road. Speeds on our highways are such that a stopped car is extremely dangerous, for oncoming drivers cannot see that it is stationary until they are almost on top of it.

Never pass on a curve or near the top of a hill; don't ever cross yellow or solid white lines. These are among the most common offenses for which police are on the lookout. They are also alert for anyone going through a red light or a Stop sign at an intersection. One can be stopped and fined for any of these faults.

Traffic lights are controlled for different speeds; in large cities these vary depending on the area, flow of traffic, and time of day. Often they are set for 25 miles per hour. If you try to find and maintain the set speed, you will "make" most lights and "flow" with the traffic. Talk to taxi drivers about this. They are experts at "making lights" and can give you many tips.

Speed Limits

Speed limits are strictly enforced, sometimes by radar, sometimes by unmarked police cars, sometimes by regular police cars which radio to one another up and down the highways.

Watch all road signs carefully as you drive along. Speed regulations change frequently at various locations. *Do what they say*. They may decrease suddenly, for example, at the approach to a small town or built-up area, a factory roadway, or a railroad. They are particularly enforced in school traffic zones, which extend on either side of any school and are posted as "School Zone." This is usually a 15-mile-per-hour area; it is essential to reduce speed drastically in such zones. Even small children cross the road by themselves. They play with balls and bicycles along the edge of the road and can be a really dangerous hazard.

Rules for People on Foot

"Jaywalking"—which either means crossing in the middle of a block or crossing against the traffic light—is illegal in most communities and you could be fined if caught. You will see many people taking chances, but do not follow their example. It is not worth it. Most pedestrian injuries are the result of jaywalking.

If you come from a left-hand drive country, be especially careful to look *both* ways for oncoming cars and have your children practice doing the same. Many people are hurt by failing to do this before stepping off the curb.

Parking Rules

When you park a car, read the signs carefully. They vary in different parts of the city, at different times of the day, on different days of the week. The only way you can know what is legal for that particular spot is to read the sign. There are no blue disk zones in the United States. Many cars are towed away each day by city police for parking violations. As cities get more crowded, this procedure is spreading and being more and more effectively carried out. It is not worth the risk. You pay for the towaway; expenses for actually retrieving the car are high; in addition you pay a heavy penalty fine. The whole thing can add up to $75! In addition you go through endless red tape, embarrassment, and inconvenience. Be careful not to park near fire hydrants, bus stops, private driveways, or too near the corner at intersections. Towaways can result from any of these parking violations as well as for being in a "No Parking" area.

The following are some familiar parking rules:

> *No Stopping* This means what it says: you cannot park *or even stop.*

No Parking	Here you may stop long enough to pick up or discharge passengers or to drop off merchandise; you can stop your car for a brief time if someone stays in the driver's seat and able to move the car if necessary.
No Standing	You may only drop people off or pick them up if you can do it quickly; you cannot wait for anyone and you cannot leave the car there while you go in to deliver a parcel or message.
Fire Hydrants	The rule is: no standing or parking within 15 feet.
Bus Stops and Taxi Stands	If you do not interfere with traffic you can pause in them briefly, but you cannot get out of the car; you must be able to move at a moment's notice.

Hitchhikers

You will often see people of either sex "thumbing" a ride, especially along the main highways. *Do not* stop for them. Unfortunately, this practice can be quite dangerous as they may not be as innocent as they look. Furthermore, in many states it is as illegal to pick up a person as to ask for rides. You can be fined quite heavily and lose your insurance for doing it.

$$ and Sense

American money can be quite confusing. The bills—or paper money—are all the same color and size. One has to look carefully to be sure he is giving out a $1 bill and not a $10 bill, for example. Furthermore, new bills stick together easily. Be sure this does not happen to you.

Coins are also confusing. This is partly because some of them have two names, partly because the size does not indicate the value. The ten-cent coin is smaller than the five-cent coin, for example. In addition all coins are silver-colored except for the penny (one cent) which is copper-colored.

COINS

1¢—penny or cent The coin of smallest value, equal to 1/100 of a dollar. It is useful for some parking meters and some sales taxes but a penny does not buy very much! Five pennies equal a nickel.

5¢—nickel Large; easily confused with the quarter.

10¢—dime Smallest of the coins, but one of the most useful. It is used for pay telephones, buying newspapers, coin-operated machines and some bus fares.

25¢—quarter This coin is larger than the nickel but easy to mistake for it. This is the normal tipping coin, also commonly used for paying bridge and road tolls.

There is also a 50¢ coin, somewhat larger than a quarter and easily recognized, and a silver dollar which is similar in size to a quarter but octagonal in shape rather than perfectly round. Be careful, the dollar (which has the image of Susan B. Anthony on it) is easily confused with the quarter.

One has to keep considerable change on hand, especially in cities which require exact change for their buses. Sales taxes also require a lot of small coins, although stores will make change. Bus drivers, however, are often not allowed to make change in many cities.

BILLS

These come in the following denominations: $1, $5, $10, and $20. They also come in $50 and $100 bills, but these are seen less often by most of us! Keep small-value bills with you. Taxi drivers, subway attendants, and some store clerks will not change anything larger than a $5 bill; most supermarket check-outs will however.

It is a good idea to get a selection of American coins and bills from your bank before leaving home and practice with them so that you can recognize them easily. If you do this with your children too, they can also become comfortable with the currency and make that adjustment before they even arrive.

There is no limit to the dollars you can bring into or take out of the United States; however, your own country may, of course, restrict the amount you may take with you. You will need to check on that before leaving home.

MONEY ON ARRIVAL

You should have with you a *minimum* of $50 of American money on arrival at a U.S. airport for tips to porters and for transportation into the city. There are money exchanges in all international airports, but it is a bother to stop at the moment of arrival when you also have to cope with luggage, crowds, fatigue, and so forth. It is better to convert an adequate supply of money before departing. Taxi fares are rising rapidly in this country and airports are generally several miles outside the city. Airport buses are *much* less expensive and are recommended unless you have a large number of people in your group or considerable luggage. The bus will take you to a central point in the city from where you can hire a cab to your final destination at far lower cost.

BANKS

Before you open a checking account, ask carefully about the various possible plans. A "Regular" account requires a specific (rather high) balance in the bank at all times, but there is no charge for each check issued. A "Special" account does not require as large a balance, but there is a charge for each check and sometimes a small monthly carrying charge as well. A "NOW" account allows you to combine a savings and checking account—and earn interest on the money that would usually be in the checking account. These are worth investigating—compare what is offered by different banks.

Unless you use 20 to 25 checks each month, a "Regular" account is not worthwhile. You would do better to put the large balance required into a savings bank and draw interest on it. (*NOTE:* Savings banks generally pay more interest than do commerical banks so they are better places to keep any sizable amounts of money. Some offer free checking; ask advice.)

The United States is becoming more and more a "cashless society". People are making purchases by check or charge account or credit card, rather than carrying too much money in their pockets or purses.

Normally people pay by check at the end of each month at department stores and some food markets and drugstores. They also pay monthly by check for rent, telephone, electricity, milk, newspaper delivery, and similar household expenses. Many have charge cards to pay for gasoline and service station expenses and credit cards for restaurant, hotel, and travel costs.

Many other people, however, prefer to pay-as-they-go and not accumulate monthly bills. Most people work out a combination, paying some bills in cash and charging others. This is a matter of personal choice. But if you have charge accounts, be *sure* to pay promptly; the interest charged for late payments can be high. Once you are recognized or have opened an account, you can use checks instead of cash at many stores.

However much money you keep on your premises or in your pocket or purse, you should be extremely careful with it. Never leave a wallet or purse on a desk in your office or on a store counter *for even a moment*. Keep them out of sight and away from the entrance hall or doorway even at home. Do not carry too much cash when you go out. Regretfully, purse-snatching and pocket-picking are quite common in metropolitan areas in the United States, as they are in other parts of the world too.

SAFE DEPOSIT BOXES

If you have jewelry or other valuables (passports, wills, stock certificates, mortgage or insurance papers, leases, and so on), you should rent a safe deposit box at a nearby bank. This will cost between $15-$250 per year depending on the size of the box and the area of the country. You can get your valuables out any time within banking hours, and these irreplaceable items will be safe and protected in bank vaults. If you are staying in a hotel, have the desk clerk put jewelry and other items into the hotel safe. *Do not leave valuables in your hotel room,* even in a suitcase. Insure jewelry, furs, expensive cameras, watches, or any items that can easily be stolen. It is worth it.

SENDING MONEY ABROAD

There are several ways to send money to someone in another country. If time is important, you may make arrangements at your bank by asking them to send a "cable transfer" to a bank in another country. If there is no urgency, banks can make less expensive transfers by letters to foreign banks. If you want the bank to notify the receiver of the funds, be sure to tell them the person's address! In order to receive such funds, the person will have to present himself at the overseas bank with proper identification.

Money can also be sent abroad through the U.S. Postal Service. (See Chapter 13.)

CHARGE ACCOUNTS AND CREDIT CARDS

Most department stores offer charge accounts; they will ask for bank and other credit references. The process of opening an account may take a number of weeks. You will be given a "charge card" when your application is approved. This makes it possible to charge purchases and minimizes the amount of cash you have to carry with you; it greatly speeds up the buying process; you can return goods and obtain a credit on your account. You generally will not get a cash refund, but your account will be credited.

The *disadvantage* of a charge account is that one must be *very* careful about the charge card. If you lose it and someone picks it up, he can run up heavy charges on your account, yet you will be held liable until you cancel the card. If you *do* lose it, call the store *immediately* and report the loss. Then *write them at once* and report it again in writing, telling them the day and hour when you phoned in to report the loss. Keep a copy of the letter. You will not be liable *after the time you first reported it.* Carry your charge cards with you only when you plan to go shopping—do not normally carry them in your purse or wallet.

Some people leave them at home, making a note of the account number. This is safer but slower, for then the salesclerk must check your number, by telephone, with each purchase. This often takes quite a while, and the waiting can be tedious.

TIPPING

This is a difficult subject. There are no absolute rules; most people give between 15 and 20 percent of the bill depending on how much service they have had, how many people have been involved, how long they have been at a place, how much they have enjoyed it, and where they are in the United States.

Fifteen percent (in big cities) indicates minimal satisfaction; 20 percent means something a bit more than that. Outside major cities, 15 percent is still the common tip.

The normal tipping coin for small services is the quarter (25¢).

People you DO tip in the United States are:

Waiters, taxi drivers, porters, doormen, hat-check girls. You also tip for personal services from barbers, shoeshine boys, beauty parlor attendants, and so on. You tip delivery people and parking lot-attendants if they have parked your car or fetched it for you.

Unfortunately many employers of these workers underpay, considering tips to be part of the wages. If one does not tip, therefore, one is harming the worker.

People you DO NOT tip include:

Customs officials or *other government employees* such as policemen or firemen. This is considered bribery.

Mailmen. You do not tip them, but you do give them a Christmas gift of $5 to $10 each (there may be several serving a large apartment house).

Airline personnel. No tips to stewards, stewardesses, or ticket agents.

Room clerks or *people at hotel desks.* (Not like the European concierge system.)

Bus drivers. Except if they also serve as guides on guided tours— then give them $1 with a "Thank you" as you leave.

Store clerks.

Gas station attendants.

Elevator operators, receptionists, or *telephone operators.*

Employees in private clubs.

Theater ushers or *movie ushers.* Programs are also free (paid for by the advertisements in them). You *do,* however, tip ushers at sports events, for some unknown reason, and you *do* pay for sports programs.

Normal Tips

There is disagreement about amounts, and tipping customs vary considerably from one part of the United States to another, as well as from small town to large city. When you are settled in your area, you should ask about this locally.

But to put newcomers at ease during their initial few days, the following suggestions are offered:

Waiters

Give at least 15 percent to the waiter. Tips are *not included* in our bills. Give the waiter more if you have asked for extras, been particularly slow, had a large group, or requested help in understanding the menu or in serving young children—that is, if you have received more than minimal service in any way.

As everywhere, tips are naturally higher in fancier restaurants. If you order wine, the wine steward may expect a tip as well as the waiter. In such a place your tip for the waiter should be not less than 20 percent.

In a low-priced restaurant, snack bar, or coffeehouse, the tip is about 25¢ for a bill of $1.25. Leave 15 to 25¢ under your plate for anything less than that. If you have just had a single cup of coffee or tea, you can leave a dime (10¢).

If you order room service in a hotel, 15-20 percent of the bill is proper.

Taxi Drivers

A quarter is enough for any fare up to $1.50; after that, give 15-20 percent. If there are several people or you have a lot of luggage, give a little more. In some cities (as in Atlanta) there is an extra charge for each passenger. Such variations are posted in the cab so you can read them.

Porters

Many air, bus or rail terminals now charge a fixed fee of 35¢ a bag. If they do, this information is posted. Otherwise, 25¢ a bag or 50¢ for a small trunk is adequate.

Doormen

For normal small daily services, you do not tip *except* if they call a taxicab. Then give them a quarter. If they help with a great deal of luggage at any time, give them 25-50¢ per bag, depending on the amount of trouble taken.

Most people give doormen occasional tips—ranging from 50¢ to $2—for any extra services they many perform or on special occasions or if they have given (and have not been tipped for) a good many small services over a considerable period of time. This is considered a "sweetener." It is not required, but it helps to keep service amiable and good!

Christmas

Christmas is special and expensive!

If you live in an apartment house where there are doormen, give each one of them a gift of $5 or more at Christmastime. The amount will vary depending on how long you have been living there, the size of your family, and how many other tips you have given throughout the year. At Christmas also the superintendent of your apartment house should be given a gift of $15 or more.

Christmas tips are normally given also to the tradespeople one sees regularly—the laundryman, newspaper boy, milkman, parking lot attendant, postman, hairdresser or barber. There is some leeway depending on how often they have served you, how friendly you are together, and your own financial level. But if you feel warmly disposed to them, $2 to $5 in a Christmas card would be much appreciated by any or all such people who have worked for you throughout the year.

Personal Services

It is hard to give a rule of thumb as to how much to tip barbers, hairdressers, delivery boys, parking lot attendants, the maid who looks after your hotel room, and all such people who serve you. Rates vary depending on the part of the country, how much service they have given, and other factors.

Best advice is to ask locally. If you cannot find anyone to ask easily, you can say directly to the person involved: "I would like to give you something for your service but I am a stranger here; what is the normal tip?"

Almost surely you will get a big smile and an honest answer.

Chapter 11

To Your Good Health

FINDING A DOCTOR

One of the first things you will need to do when you settle into your house or apartment is to find a doctor and get on his "list." This should be done *before* you or anyone in your family needs medical care. Doctors in this country are so busy that all too often people have real trouble in getting help when they need it if they have not made a prior connection with a physician. You may be lucky enough to find someone who will see you at a moment's notice, but a doctor's first obligation is to his own patients. If he is very busy, a newcomer who is not on his list may have to wait a good while. It is far better to become one of his patients before any crisis arises.

General practitioners—or family doctors—are becoming increasingly rare; as medicine gets more and more complicated, doctors tend more and more to specialties. Those physicians known as "internists"—meaning internal ailments—are now taking the place of family doctors in many areas. If your trouble falls into some other category, the doctor will refer you to the proper specialist and make the connection for you.

Many medical groups have formed which give the patient access to a number of doctors rather than one. They emphasize family practice—taking care of all the medical needs of family members in one place but still do not usually go to people's homes.

How do you go about finding a reliable doctor whom you can afford? It is not easy, and it usually takes a bit of time. Don't necessarily accept the first physician suggested. People have different needs. Do you care most about top-level technical competence? Or is it important to you for your doctor to have a gentle personality and to be willing to give you considerable time? Are costs of primary importance to you, or is it vital that the doctor come to the house? (By no means will all doctors do this—it too is becoming increasingly rare in this country.)

There is a variety of ways to search. Your company may advise you. Often there is a company doctor, or they may have connections with a medical "group." This is a great help. Perhaps you will ask your neighbors or the person from whom you rent your apartment, or the head of your child's school. The officer at the bank or your church minister may also give you advice as to someone you can trust. Your own consulate may have a list of doctors who speak your language.

Failing a personal recommendation from someone you know, call the County Medical Society in your area. The Society can either provide a list of doctors who are taking patients or tell you where you can get this information. When you have found an internist whose age, medical training, and background seem right to you, make an appointment to see him. Take him your family's health records and ask about his range of fees, his hospital connections, whether or not he makes house visits, and anything else you want to know. This is your chance to decide about him; it is the time he gets to know you and your needs. He will, of course, bill you for the visit, but it is worth it.

If such an approach seems unsatisfactory to you, you can call the administrator's office at the nearest hospital. Ask the secretary to tell you the office addresses of two or three of the newest internists who have been given "privileges" at that hospital. This way you will find well-trained men with a nearby hospital affiliation. If they are either young or new to the neighborhood, they are probably not yet swamped with more patients than they can handle, so they will be able to take on a new family.

In America, hospitals are the best criteria for continued medical competence. If a doctor is on the staff of a really good hospital, he is under pressure to keep his medical knowledge and ability up to date. Therefore you can place your confidence in him.

Don't feel shy about discussing fees when you first make these contacts. They vary widely and it is better to know in advance the range of price for any given physician.

As we have said before, be braced for high costs, especially in large cities where high overhead is passed on to the patients in doctor's bills.

General Advice

For routine medical care, look for a young doctor who has had good medical training but has not had the time to develop a heavy work load. He will probably give you more attention and charge less. If the problem is technically difficult, you (or he) can and will consult a specialist anyway.

EMERGENCIES

If an emergency strikes and you have no doctor—or the one you have is unavailable—take the patient yourself by car or taxi directly to the Emergency Room of the nearest hospital. It is a good idea to make a mental note of where this is as soon as you arrive. Some people post a note by their telephone, listing emergency addresses and telephone numbers. In most of the country the emergency number for ambulance, police, or fire is 911; but it is well to check this locally. If you do not know the emergency number, just dial "0" for the operator and tell her your situation. If you do this, *do not forget to give your address.* Many a person has hung up without doing this and thereby wasted precious moments while the operator has had to call back—and sometimes been unable to trace the call.

IF YOU ARE SENT TO A HOSPITAL

Although health care is unbelievably expensive in the United States, it is good and in most cases very thorough. People are sent to hospitals more often here than in many other countries. If this happens to you, don't fear the worst! It often only means that the doctor wants to make use of special facilities for tests, X-ray, or treatment procedures, or that he wants to have you observed at frequent intervals over a period of days by a trained staff. Don't be frightened. It does not necessarily mean that he thinks you are seriously ill.

HEALTH INSURANCE

Since medical costs are so high, insurance is *necessary*. There are many excellent free public facilities for the poor, but they are so crowded and the waiting time is so long that most people who can afford it use private medicine. As yet there is no national system of health insurance like those in many other countries of the world (except for Medicare which covers only persons over 65 years of age).

In lieu of this, the great majority of the American people subscribe to *private* insurance programs which help to pay for hospital and doctor bills. You should join such a program too. If you work for an American enterprise, it is quite likely that there is a group insurance plan to which you and your family will automatically belong, but you should find out about this in detail. If there is such a plan, payments are made through automatic payroll deductions. Find out exactly what the coverage includes since this varies from one plan to another. Is maternity care included? What about dental coverage? surgery? eye care? pediatrics? psychiatry?

If you are working for an organization which does not have group insurance, you *most certainly* should purchase private health insurance for yourself and your family. One bad accident could cost you more than you own. Most insurance plans are open to international personnel after they have been U.S. residents for six months; a few will cover them earlier than that.

Foreign students enrolled in U.S. colleges and universities pay their college infirmary fee and are entitled to receive infirmary care whenever they need it. They can also purchase additional low-cost accident insurance—which is advised and often required. The university or college catalogue will give details. Families of students, however, are *not* eligible for infirmary care and should be covered with outside health insurance.

Medical Insurance never covers all expenses. Read the policy carefully and have someone explain it to you in detail. Coverage varies widely from one policy to another. Usually they do *not* include drugs and medicines, dental care, eyeglasses, or doctors' visits to the home. You can have these specialties added, but the cost rises sharply with each one. Be sure to think over carefully exactly what you really need, balancing the cost of the policy against those services you could afford to cover yourself.

Before selecting a health insurance agent, it is a good idea to obtain advice from a colleague or friend. Most agents are reliable, but some are not; you will need help in selecting a reputable firm.

Paying Hospital Bills

Be prepared to pay all hospital bills before taking the patient home. Your corporation or your insurance may cover such matters for you; otherwise the hospital is likely to demand full payment—even if this requires your taking out a loan to cover it. It is advisable to talk to your employer, your doctor, or your insurance agent about this so you will know your own situation before an emergency arises.

BEFORE YOU LEAVE HOME

Bring your family's health records with you if you can. This may save on expensive tests or background studies. Also, have full dental attention before you leave home; costs for dentistry as well as medical care are extremely high in the United States.

If you wear eyeglasses, have an extra pair with you, and be sure to bring a copy of the prescription.

Chapter 12

Food and Food Customs

HOTELS

Most people start their visit to the United States by staying in a hotel. You will find that hotel restaurants, grills, lounges, and so on, are nearly always more expensive than neighborhood restaurants. In addition, hotel food is sometimes not especially good and hotel dining rooms are sometimes dull. It is worth wandering up and down the nearby streets to see if you cannot find something less expensive and more fun. The words "coffee shop" in a hotel (or airport) mean that prices are more reasonable than in a restaurant. "Snack bars" are even cheaper, but you may have to stand at the counter or sit in a booth.

RESTAURANTS

Because America is home to so many different nationalities, one can find almost any kind of restaurant in practically all the larger cities. Listings in the classified telephone directory may be by nationality or by area of the city or both, and range widely in price. Many post their menus in the window so you can get an idea of prices before you enter. If not, you may want to ask to see a menu before you get really settled or else just ask about the price range. Appearances from the outside can be deceptive as to price—what looks small and inconspicuous may turn out to be very expensive, or a nice-looking place may be quite moderate. It works both ways. You can get a solid meal for about $3.00 or slightly more if you eat in snack bars, chain restaurants, or drugstores, but in a medium-

113

priced city restaurant you should expect to pay $10 to $12 per person for a nicely served dinner—with wine or drinks extra. Prices in big cities go "upward" fast!

RESERVATIONS

If you are going to a middle- or upper-level restaurant to dine, telephone ahead for a reservation—the earlier the better. Keep to the time you have given or else phone to say you will be late. Good restaurants will not hold reservations for more than a short time. If you are turned away or asked to wait because you have not reserved ahead, don't take it personally. It happens all the time. The management has no choice. Fire laws are extremely strict about the number of occupants, and unannounced fire inspections are frequent. No restaurateur dares overcrowd his establishment.

CAFETERIAS—LUNCH COUNTERS—DINERS

These are quick and cheap. The food and handling are inspected regularly by government officials so you can feel safe, although you are advised to choose a clean-looking place nonetheless. These places are crowded with people at normal mealtimes, but if you eat a little early or a little late, you can usually get a seat without waiting too long. They abound everywhere, are open long hours, and are useful in keeping your food budget down.

Diners—which look somewhat like railroad cars—are often found on the outskirts of towns. They vary from clean and shiny to rather bedraggled. Truck drivers often stop at them because they are apt to have good parking facilities. Many motorists do too. Diners serve large portions of good, filling food at low prices; furthermore, there is often an interesting cross section of people in them, especially in the early morning hours when the long-distance truck drivers are eating breakfast.

You do not generally tip at cafeterias where you serve yourself, nor is tipping required at a lunch counter, although most people leave some small change under their plate when they leave.

Fast food shops (where a limited menu is pre-cooked and ready for rapid dispensing and quick consumption) have become very widespread and popular in the U.S. Such chains as McDonald's (hamburgers and french fries), Kentucky Fried Chicken, Arby's (roast beef) cater to millions of people who want quick service, edible food in clean, simple surroundings. There is no tipping, though in many cases you are expected to clear your own table and discard your trash in the cans provided! Fast food shops are especially appealing to children and young people.

DRUG STORES

Far into the night, you can sit at a counter in some drugstores and get coffee, tea, or cocoa, sandwiches, soups, ice cream, soft drinks, and sometimes hamburgers or hot dogs. Most of them do not serve real meals, although some do.

BARS

American bars are less full of camaraderie than are bars in many other countries—no dart throwing or other games; rarely a pretty barmaid; people seldom toast each other or offer a "drink all around." U.S. bars are more often dark, quite dismally dignified.

It is a good idea to name your brand of alcohol if you care about this. Otherwise you are likely to get a cheap "house" brand.

Don't order beer by the "pint" or "half pint." Ask for a glass (usually 8 to 10 ounces) of draft or a bottle. American beer is usually light and served very cold. Imported beers, mostly European, are generally available also. Japanese beer is beginning to appear in the main cities.

U.S. whiskey tends to be sweeter, more full-bodied, and cheaper than the whiskeys of Scotland or Ireland. Canadian whiskey is light.

The main U.S. whiskeys are bourbon (made from corn) or a blend of several grains incorrectly called "rye" or simply called "blended whiskey." If you want the real "rye," be sure the bartender understands. He will generally serve the mixture unless you make your desire clear.

If you like your drink at room temperature, be sure to say "no ice." Americans like most of their drinks ice cold.

HOURS OF MEALS

It is possible to be served a meal at any hour—including all night—in most large cities. Many restaurants close on Sunday, but many others are open. Chains such as Horn and Hardart, McDonald's, and Howard Johnson are found in the telephone book. These usually list certain locations which are open on Sundays.

Some places offer Sunday "Brunch" (or you might be invited to a "Brunch" at someone's house). This is a combination of breakfast and lunch, served about 11:30 or twelve o'clock for late Sunday sleepers.

If you are outside a major city, it may be difficult to find a place that is open after 8:30 or 9:00 P.M., though lunch counters, diners, fast food shops and drugstores usually stay open late.

In people's homes there is considerable variety as to eating times. Around cities the main meal is usually served in the evening, but in rural areas it may be eaten in the middle of the day. In commuting areas, dinner is often quite late because of train schedules. In cities people normally eat dinner about 7:00 or 7:30 if they have cocktails, earlier if they do not. Throughout the country most people dine relatively early—6:30 P.M. is quite common. The hour for parties is usually later.

FINDING OUT WHERE TO GO

Most cities feature a multitude of inexpensive paperback books covering their eating places; local magazines and newspapers carry advertisements; there are lists of national restaurants which run the gamut of price and elegance. The best thing to do is to browse in the local bookstore to find a book which indicates price ranges, and then go explore! Your colleagues at work will be glad to offer suggestions too, both pro and con.

AMERICAN FOOD HABITS

Generally speaking, American food is rather bland and unspiced. Salads are much liked and are served all year round. Many people in this sedentary country are trying to keep down their weight and so they are "calorie" conscious. This is evident in menus offering "low calorie" or "weight watchers" meals. In markets one can find "No Cal" drinks (meaning without calories) such as ginger ale or cola. "Diet" foods without sugar or salt are also available in food stores. You need not bother with these shelves, but you may be interested in knowing they are there.

Waiters in restaurants tend to assume that everyone drinks coffee, but you do not have to do so! If he suddenly says "Now or later?" what he means is "Do you want coffee with your meal or later?" Many—but by no means all—Americans drink coffee or tea *with* their meal. Either way is perfectly acceptable. When dining out, you can ask for tea, milk, coke, beer, and so on, if you prefer these to coffee. Restaurants cannot serve beer, wine, or liquor unless they are licensed to do so. Normally when eating in a home it is considered better manners to take whatever is being served and not to ask for something different—unless the hostess gives you a choice.

The main course in American meals is usually meat, fowl, or fish, but rarely is more than one of these served at the same meal (except that seafood can be used as an appetizer—shrimp cocktail, pickled herring, oysters, etc.).

Most North Americans eat quickly during the day—that is, breakfast and lunch—unless it is a social, business, or family occasion. The evening meal, however, is usually leisurely and a family time. Racing through daytime meals is part of the "pace" described earlier; working time is considered precious. There is also another reason—namely, the ever-present pressure of time and people. Others in public eating places are waiting for you to finish so they too can be served and get back to work within the allotted time. Each one hurries to make room for the next person.

There is a real difference in leisure and timing here when a meal is "social," meaning shared and enjoyed, or when it is "just a meal."

A LANGUAGE ALL ITS OWN

Meat

If you order steaks, chops, hamburgers, and so on, the waiter may look at you blankly and say: "How d'ya want it?" What he means is: rare? medium? well done?

"Rare" is likely to be *very* rare; "well done" to be very well done. If you prefer, you can indicate something in the middle by saying "medium rare" or "medium well done."

Coffee

If you are asked "Regular?" when you order, this means "Do you want lots of cream in it?" If not, ask for "black" (no cream) or "dark" (meaning a small amount of cream). Often the cream is brought separately, and you add your own—but not always. The "cream," by the way, is almost always milk.

Coffee is the usual American drink at all hours of the day. It varies enormously in quality; you will just have to experiment to find places that make it the way you like it. Espresso is often available, but one has to ask for it.

Tea

Tea is much less popular in the United States than coffee —perhaps because it is often quite poor (perhaps we make it poorly because we don't drink it as much as other nationalities do). In public places tea is usually a shock to the newcomer. A cup of hot water (no longer boiling if it ever was) is brought in with a limp tea bag in the saucer. You are supposed to put the bag into the water and leave it there until the tea is as strong as you like it. In private homes one will generally find it better made than this!

Other Drinks

Next after coffee, Americans are likely to drink coke, or other soft drinks, milk shakes or other milk drinks, or fruit juices. Iced tea is apt to be good and is widely drunk in summer, as is iced coffee. If you want to drink water, you will probably have to ask for it. It is safe anywhere.

Bread and Butter

These are usually served in restaurants whether or not you ask for them; there is no charge for them.

Eggs

Boiled eggs are broken into cups—rarely, if ever, eaten out of the shell. Fried may be "sunny-side up," meaning fried on one side only (with the yellow face showing), "over," meaning well fried on both sides, or "over easy," meaning fried lightly on both sides.

The waiter at a restaurant will ask you: "How do you want your eggs?" Your answer can include any one of wide range of possibilities: boiled, fried, scrambled, or poached; with or without ham or bacon or sausage. You also indicate the number of eggs you want. Many Americans consider two normal.

Additional prices for one or two slices of bacon or a sausage or two may be out of all proportion. Take a look at the price on the menu before ordering.

French Fries and "Slaw"

"French fries" are fried potatoes—like British "chips." You often get them with a meal whether you order them or not. The same is true of small paper cups of cole slaw—sliced cabbage and mayonaise. If these are served with the meal, there is no extra charge for them.

Hot Dogs or "Franks"

Usually these are eaten in a long bread roll. They can be either beef or pork. You have your choice of adding tomato ketchup (spiced tomato sauce), mustard, pickle, relish, or onion (sliced and raw). Some people put all of these on at once! There is no charge for such condiments.

The special language of the "short order" cook behind a lunch counter is a mystery even to Americans. Orders such as "draw one" or "shoot one" mean "pour a cup of coffee" or "pour a glass of Coke"; "B.L.T." means a "bacon, lettuce, and tomato" sandwich. If you hear "B.L.T. down," this means "on white toast"! You do not have to *know* this language, but it is amazing to listen to it as you sit at a busy counter. Feel free to *order* in normal terms however. The man serving you does not expect you to use his jargon!

Chapter 13

Getting in Touch with People

POSTAL SERVICE

Mail service in the United States is expensive, poor, and often incredibly slow, especially in the large cities, where millions of pieces are handled by antiquated equipment. Deliveries are made normally only once a day, but not on Sundays.

For ordinary mail within the United States, buy a "roll" of 100 of the required stamp plus a supply of air letter forms for overseas. If you have such supplies for your normal daily needs, you can then drop your letters into the nearest mailbox and avoid standing in long lines at the post office. If you must go to the post office, try to avoid the lunch hour or the four to five o'clock rush when every mailing clerk in the city is bringing in the day's office mail.

In the U.S., zip codes follow the name of the city and state; they do not precede as in Europe, South America and other places.

Sending Money Abroad

If you want to forward money by postal order, be sure to ask for an *international* form. Many a person has mistakenly sent the domestic one which cannot be cashed abroad. You must specify this clearly.

Registry

If you want to be sure an important letter has been received, send it "Registered, with Return Receipt Requested."

Most personal mail goes first class. Other classes of mail cover advertisements, magazines, and so forth. If you are interested in anything besides the usual first class postage, ask at the post office for "Special Delivery" (delivered by hand), "Insured Mail," or rates on mailing "In Bulk."

Parcels

There are many rules and regulations governing the mailing of packages. Permissable sizes and weights vary. Some *must* be sealed, and others may not be sealed but *must* be tied with string (so they can be opened for inspection). You are advised to ask at the post office (by telephone if you like) before you wrap a parcel for shipment abroad so as to save yourself the nuisance of having to take it home and begin again.

Never include anything written in a package. If you get caught doing so, you can be fined. Written materials—even short notes— are supposed to go by the more expensive first class mail. If you want the note to arrive with the parcel, put it in an ordinary envelope with the proper first class stamp, fasten the envelope to the parcel with gummed tape or glue, and write clearly on it: "Letter Inside." The recipient will be sure to notice it then and not think it is merely a label.

There are special rates for books and printed matter. Ask the postal clerk about this.

United Parcel Service (UPS) is taking over much parcel delivery within the U.S., being both cheaper and quicker in many cases. It is worth calling them for any large parcels (see phone book for addresses). They will pick up parcels from your house or office though, of course, charge for doing so.

Also inquire about Federal Express and other expensive but quick methods of sending mail.

TELEPHONES

The United States is a telephone land. Almost everyone uses the telephone to make or break social engagements, to say their "Thank you's," to do their shopping and ordering (even from food and drug stores), and to obtain all kinds of information. Telephones save your feet and endless amounts of time—not to mention multiple bus or subway fares! Do get used to using the phone readily. It is the chief means of communication in the United States. Some visitors from other countries hesitate at first either because it is unfamiliar or because they are afraid that they will be "intruding" or "bothering" the other person. Within normal hours—after eight in the morning and before nine at night (but not at mealtimes)—people are used to the telephone ringing and will not mind at all. All offices have an employee whose job it is to answer the phone. You need never worry about calling a business concern for information, nor will you find them closed at lunchtime, though of course a particular individual may be out.

It is simple and quick to have a phone installed. Just call the Business Office of the Telephone Company (see the Directory). They will install it on a specific day by appointment, when it is convenient for you. You must be at home to tell them where you want it placed. (All this is barring strikes or emergencies, of course.)

Although you will be offered a multitude of extra services and a variety of fancy phones, just ask for the basic installation. Color, fancy shapes, push buttons, and so on, all cost more, not once, but every month thereafter. They are not necessary. Second extensions may be useful in big or busy houses and are not expensive; but other extras *are* expensive and hardly worth the cost for most people.

You will be charged a basic monthly rate which includes a fixed number of local calls. Calls beyond that number or for longer distances will be added to the monthly bill. You can send telegrams and cables from your home telephone; these too will appear on your telephone bill at the end of the month.

When your telephone is installed, you will be given two directories—the regular directory, in which names of people with phones are listed alphabetically, and the Classified Directory (often called "The Yellow Pages" for obvious reasons). It is worthwhile to sit down and really study both these books when you first get them. They contain a great deal of information about using the telephone, special services that are available (including time, weather, or traffic information), rates, times of the week when one can phone most cheaply, and so on. The "Classified" lists all businesses, organizations, restaurants, stores, and services in your area in such a way that you can quickly find whatever you need. If you study that directory, you will learn much about your city and the range of what is available. For example the schools, clubs, organizations, public swimming pools; all kinds of instruction and classes; where to buy special foods or spices; where to have repairs made on all sorts of goods; restaurants by nationality; places where you can *rent* television sets, records, children's cribs, crutches, fur coats or a wide range of articles (look under "Rental Service").

The Classified Directory, which is corrected and updated every year, can become one of your best friends if you take the trouble to get to know it well. In smaller towns, the regular and classified directories are in a single volume.

Telephone Credit Cards

As soon as you have your own telephone—and therefore your own number—you can call the Business Office of the Telephone Company and ask for a Credit Card. This is free and a great convenience. It enables you to make calls or send cables from any telephone, public or private, and have the call charged to your home account. This often saves you from having to struggle with exact change in a telephone booth or makes it possible to call from a friend's home or office without imposing on his generosity.

Public Telephones

Different countries put their public telephones in different places. Here they are widespread. You will find them in bus and air terminals, railroad stations, stores, hotels, the lobbies of many office buildings, restaurants, gasoline stations, and in small booths along streets and highways. Instructions for use are found on each phone. Long-distance and overseas calls can also be made from public telephones, but they require a handful of change in nickels, dimes, and quarters. If you would like the recipient to pay the charges, ask the operator to make it a "collect" call. You can ask the operator what the charges will be for a three-minute call before you place it. If you ask her to do so, she will tell you when your three minutes are up. You can talk longer, but must pay another charge. All operator services cost extra.

Two Types of Long-Distance Calls

One can make calls either "person -to-person" or "station-to-station." "Person-to-person" is far more expensive, but you only pay charges from the time you actually begin speaking to the person you ask for and no charge if the person is not there. If you are uncertain of his/her being there and are calling from a long distance, this is worthwhile. In "station-to-station" calls, you start to pay from the moment the call goes through, no matter who answers. This is the better method, for it is much cheaper, if you think your person is likely to be there or if you merely want to leave a message.

TELEGRAMS AND CABLES

The Western Union Company handles telegrams and cables in the United States and overseas, but they are not recommended for fast, reliable service. It is better to *telephone* anything urgent in the States or to use I.T.T. (International Telephone and Telegraph) or R.C.A. for cables abroad. Both R.C.A. and I.T.T. offer Full Rate Telegrams (called FR), which are the fastest; Letter Telegrams (LT), which is an overnight service; and Telex Transmission, which is charged by the minute, not by the word, and is useful to those who send a volume of international telegrams. Look up either company in the phone book or send your message through Western Union with the words "Via ITT" or "Via RCA" after the address.

None of these are sent from the post office as they are in many other countries. You send them via telephone. If you must send a cable from a pay telephone, ask the operator the charges in advance so you can be sure to have the correct change. A credit card is a blessing in such a case. Rates are based on the number of words. The names and addresses of persons sending and receiving the message are not counted as part of the message within the United States, but in cables or radiograms going overseas, they are.

There are various types of local messages.

The "straight" telegram:

This is the quickest but most expensive. It allows 15 words for the minimum charge.

The Night Letter:

This is the least expensive, but slowest, being held for delivery until the following morning.

The Day Letter:

This falls between the two, taking longer than a straight telegram but being delivered during the same day. This allows 50 words (rather than 15) for its minimum charge.

Chapter 14

Safety and Emergencies

Everyone knows that cities grow ever more violent and full of trouble; however, one need not live scared. If one follows certain normal procedures, minds one's own business, and stays away from dark, unsavory places, the chances of having a misfortune—while not totally removed—are very much diminished.

ON THE STREETS

Keep to the more traveled and better-lit streets after dark. If you have to move through dangerous areas, go by bus or taxi. Try to board your bus in a populated area so you do not have to wait at a bus stop in a deserted locality.

Avoid parks after dark; walk on the nonpark side of the street if you are passing a park. People with bad intent often loiter in dark places. They like the edges of parks because they can make a quick escape. They also like doorways and alleys. If one feels apprehensive, one walks, therefore, on the curb side of the sidewalk.

If you have to wait in a train or bus terminal at night, do so in the main waiting room where it is light and people are passing, or else choose a place in sight of a guard or policeman.

Avoid subway travel in evenings or at night when those subterranean tunnels are likely to be fairly deserted.

Not all—but most—crime in the United States takes place in dark, rather predictable places where there are few people about. Reasonable precautions such as the above markedly reduce one's chance of trouble.

SECURITY AT HOME

Locks only work if you use them! Never leave the door to your house or apartment unlocked; be careful not to leave a key in the door by mistake even for a short while; don't leave your door open, ajar, or unlocked even if you are just going out to empty the trash or talk with a neighbor. Especially at night, it is a good precaution to keep the inside chain on the door.

Most city apartments have "peepholes" through which you can see who is at your door before you open it. Others have TV systems in the front lobby or some voice identification arrangement. *Use whatever system is provided.* It is there for your protection. If you live near the ground floor or facing a fire escape and are worried about your windows, talk to the superintendent about window locks or extra metal screens.

Don't open a door until you know who is there. Don't admit a salesman, a repairman, or a delivery boy unless you have ordered from them or are expecting them. Be *sure* of who is at your door before you open it. Many service people carry identification cards issued to them by their companies. Ask to see it.

None of this is meant to frighten you, but it is just common sense. If you use the various safeguards that exist, then you can feel secure, relaxed, and protected. If you do not, you are taking a chance nowadays anywhere.

Should you lock yourself out of your apartment by mistake, the superintendent can let you in again. He will have a master key for such emergencies. Some people also leave a spare key with a trusted neighbor for just such moments of need.

It is nice to know that in most large cities there are locksmiths available on 24-hour duty. Look under "Locksmiths" in the Classified Directory. Such a man can be a lifesaver if, for example, you break off the key in your car lock after a party some night!

FIRE

There are some simple precautions that will help prevent fires. Do *no* burning of trash on your own. Most populated areas of the country have laws that forbid trash burning by individuals. Trash is placed in cans or strong plastic bags for pickup by the garbage collectors. In apartment houses, follow the trash instructions for the building. Never leave your home—even for a minute—while anything is cooking, especially in oil.

Most fires are caused by burning fat or by defective electrical wiring or by cigarettes. All homes should have a small foam fire extinguisher near the stove; these are good for either fat or electrical fires. You can buy small portable ones at most hardware stores. *Be sure to check the date on it before you buy*—they deteriorate with age. Baking soda quickly smothers grease or oil flames. Smoke alarms are inexpensive, easily installed and good warnings, especially at night. They are also available in most hardware stores.

The *phone number to call* when you detect a fire is prominently listed in local phone directories. This number should be posted beside each phone in your home. If a fire *does* break out, call this number or dial "0" for operator and tell the person who answers *where the fire is.* In an apartment building, call the building superintendent, doorman, or elevator operator *immediately,* however small the fire is.

INSURANCE

You might think this subject need not concern you. Unfortunately there is a growing need for everyone to carry liability insurance because an increasing number of people are claiming high damages after even the simplest and most ordinary of accidents. If someone trips on your front step, or your dog knocks over a child, or your cleaning woman gets burned on your stove, they could—and a growing number do—enter a lawsuit against you and claim damages out of all proportion. Courts assume that one is covered by insurance, and so they often award far more in "damages" than would seem reasonable to most of us. If you do *not* carry insurance for such a situation, you can be in bad financial trouble.

The term to use when inquiring is "comprehensive liability." An insurance agent will advise you about the proper level of coverage for your income, the size of your family, and so on. Be sure to consult a responsible agent who will not sell you more insurance than you need. You should find him through your firm or someone you know in a bank, or a friend, or a lawyer. Then talk freely with him. When you get the agent's advice, it is a good idea to "double-check" by discussing what has been recommended with a colleague or friend before actually signing any contract. Never let the agent rush you; the more he tries to, the more cautious you should be.

You should also seek advice on other kinds of insurance according to the value of your possessions and property. If you did not bring any jewelry, fine paintings, or furniture, you may not need to carry such property insurance as fire or theft, but you should discuss this carefully with a knowledgeable person who can judge in relation to your belongings. Insurance is expensive. One can easily be talked into "overinsuring" goods that could be replaced without too much trouble if they were lost. You will never receive the full value from your insurance anyway. Often it works out to be a very small percentage of the value. The fine print on the contract is confusing, but extremely important. Do get someone who understands contracts to go over yours with you in detail.

Generally speaking, you need cover only a few selected, expensive, and irreplaceable material possessions (such as jewels, furs, or cameras, for example) for theft, but in addition you need to be well covered against liability, in case of being sued; you need adequate health and accident insurance because medical costs are so high here (see Chapter 10); and you need substantial auto insurance if you plan to drive (see Chapter 8).

Part III

For Those Who Stay Longer

Chapter 15

Housing

HOW TO BEGIN LOOKING

As is true in large cities throughout the world, the farther out from any urban center, generally the lower the rents will be. However, transportation may be so overcrowded and expensive that one has to balance these two factors in deciding where to settle. Naturally it is easier to take part in the life of a city if one is close to the center. For this reason single people or childless couples usually prefer not to live too far out. However, families with children generally tend to settle in the suburbs. They do so in search of larger houses at lower rents, less crowded schools, and a slower pace—not to mention grass and trees!

If your children are of school age, the quality of local schools should be of primary concern *before you decide on any home*. Many families have found that in the end it was cheaper to move to a fairly expensive suburb which had good public schools rather than a cheaper neighborhood where inadequate or crowded public schools forced them to send their children to costly private schools. If there are many children in a family, this is particularly important to consider.

Once the school question has been looked into, commuting conditions should be investigated. Some directions out from each city are likely to be easier than others—better train or bus schedules, less crowded routes, more alternatives, shorter trips, and so on.

Your employer should be able to give you helpful advice about schools and commuter schedules in various areas that surround the city. You will be able to judge a good deal for yourself by driving through a number of neighborhoods. Stop and chat with people you see outside their houses; talk to the librarian or the man who runs the drugstore or the village market; investigate and "feel out" a neighborhood if you possibly can before you actually select one. Towns vary greatly even when situated next to each other.

If you are moving to a medium sized (about 500,000 population) or small city (about 100,000 population) or to a smaller town, the housing situation will be quite different from that in large metropolitan areas. Neighborhoods within these city limits may be as spacious as those in the suburbs although houses will often be older. Public transportation, however, is frequently limited in smaller cities.

SOURCES OF INFORMATION

Your best source of information about either houses or apartments is likely to be the local paper. As a rule the week's most complete real estate section appears in the Sunday edition. Try to get a copy on *Saturday!* Usually the real estate section is printed early; the local newsstand may be able to sell you one even if you have to stay up late into the evening to buy it. Time is important as there is often tremendous competition for housing. You need to do your combing of the columns the night before so that on Sunday morning you can telephone early to any likely looking prospects. You can start telephoning as early as 7 A.M.

There are real estate agents in all localities. These can be helpful, but if you can find a house yourself through friends or the newspaper or by seeing a "For Rent" sign, it is far better. Agents charge steep fees—a month's rent is common, sometimes 10 percent of the year's rent. Some companies pay such fees for their employees; others do not. Be certain you understand your company's policy regarding this matter, or else inquire about fees before you sign with any real estate agency.

IF YOU RENT A HOUSE

In addition to the rent, you will generally be expected to pay for gas and electricity, heat and hot water, and simple electrical and plumbing repairs.

You also provide and/or pay for normal maintenance such as grass-cutting, window-washing, leaf-raking, and snow removal. If the house has a sidewalk, you (not the town) are responsible for having it clear of snow within a few hours after each snowfall (usually four daylight hours).

FURNISHED APARTMENTS OR HOUSES

The word "furnished" means different things to different people. You will normally be supplied with the essentials: stove, refrigerator, beds, chairs, sofa, tables, lamps. Minimal china and glass, flatware (often rather poor), basic kitchen supplies, curtains, some pictures may be supplied. Sometimes, but very rarely, there is a small supply of bed, bath, and table linens and blankets.

You will need to supply: your favorite kitchen utensils, some table linens or mats, extra lamps, coat hangers, whatever electrical appliances you want—such as toasters, irons, etc., generally also bath and bed linens and blankets. You certainly will want to bring enough of your own things to make you feel familiar and comfortable. Your own pictures, books, sofa cushions, and the like will make it seem more like "home" to you.

TO BRING OR NOT TO BRING?

When you realize how expensive it is to ship household goods, you will agree that it often makes better sense to buy basic equipment here such as dishes, sheets, towels, saucepans, etc., rather than to ship your own unless, of course, your company is assuming all shipping costs.

Furthermore, you may want to think carefully about bringing any pieces you cherish such as that delicate clock, an antique desk, your prized elephant tusk chair. The best rule to follow is: *If the item were lost or broken, would you grieve? Or could you accept the insurance money and not care too deeply?*

Picture for yourself the crate being lifted by a ship's crane and then dropped into the ship's hold or riding out a monsoon on a dock. Probably neither of these things will happen to your things. Most goods today are packed to survive, but think about such hazards. You may decide to leave home your most valued possessions!

One more guideline: What will the climate be like in that part of the United States to which you are going? If you will be in sunny California, hot Arizona, or moist Florida, you should consider leaving heavy rugs, big upholstered chairs, velvet draperies, and the like at home. In hot areas it is practical to use rattan, glass, wicker, and so on, to leave most floors uncovered and to use louvers or shutters rather than draperies at the windows.

WHAT DO THE RENTAL WORDS MEAN?

Even "native" Americans are confused by the terms used in real estate advertisements. A tiny hallway, an alcove off the kitchen, or an "L" in the living room may be called a "room." Sometimes kitchens and bathrooms are counted as rooms, and sometimes they are not. When you see "2½ rooms" listed, you cannot be certain what this means. Neither can Americans! The only safe thing to do is to ask in each case: "Exactly what rooms are included in this apartment?" Ask to see a floor plan. Ask the sizes of the rooms. Floor plans can make a place look larger than in fact it is—and far more glamorous! Apartments are more expensive as you go higher in a building. You are paying for more light and less dirt and noise from the street.

HOUSING AGREEMENTS

Don't sign any agreement until you have consulted a member of your company's personnel department, or a lawyer, or a real estate man at your bank, a well-recommended real estate agent, or an official at your university.

You should understand clearly *in advance* what the lease says about: ending the lease; renewing it if you want to stay longer; provisions for damages; number of occupants; rules about children or pets; whether or not you can sublet; when the next price rise will occur and what it is likely to be; painting or redecoration regulations; hidden charges—sometimes extra ones suddenly appear for such items as a TV aerial, garbage removal, or a fee for a night watchman.

Rents are payable one month in advance, on the first day of each month. When you lease an apartment, you are normally asked for one month's "security deposit" in addition to the first month's rent. This will be returned to you when you leave if there has been no major damage to the premises during your occupancy. The landlord or his agent will do the inspecting. This is not the last month's rent; it is an assurance to the landlord that if you damage the premises he will be covered. For your own protection, you should examine the apartment carefully *before* you sign a lease and get the landlord's or his agent's signed (written) acknowledgement for any breaks, cracks, stains, or other damages that existed before you became the tenant. Otherwise you may be charged with these two or three years later when you leave.

If you should be transferred before your lease runs out, you will have to negotiate with the landlord to end your responsibility unless this provision is already written into your original lease.

You may have to pay the rent until he can find another tenant.

All such matters should be discussed in advance. Be *sure* to get professional legal advice before signing your name to anything. Once a contract is signed, it becomes binding. It cannot be canceled and the terms cannot be changed without the greatest legal difficulty. Furthermore, you will then have no leeway for any further negotiations.

And so, to summarize, before you sign:

1. Be sure you know which services and utilities are or are not included in the rent—electricity, gas, air conditioning, TV antenna, washing machine, etc.

2. Determine whether or not you have to pay a brokerage fee (if you found the apartment through an agent). If so, how much will it be?

3. How often will the landlord repaint the apartment? Will he pay for the painting or will you?

4. Exactly how long does the lease run? (They vary.)

5. What are the conditions under which you can end the lease if you should be transferred?

6. If you should want to sublet to someone else, can you? Under what conditions?

7. Does the landlord know the size of your family? Not all apartment houses allow children. Does this one?

8. Not all apartment houses allow pets. Have *written* permission if you are going to keep a pet.

UTILITIES—GAS, ELECTRICITY, HEAT, AIR CONDITIONING, AND WATER

In most large cities stoves burn what is called "city gas". In country areas bottled gas is often used for stoves. Some people prefer electric stoves, even though they are slower to heat, because the heat is considered more even.

Most U.S. heating systems today are oil burners operated by electric motors or else coal furnaces.

Modern apartment buildings are nearly always equipped with centrally operated air conditioning which can be adjusted by the occupants of each apartment. If you live in an older house, it is likely to have window air conditioners. If there are no window units and the need is great, one can rent air conditioners on a monthly basis for the few hot months.

Normally fees for gas and electricity are *not* included in the monthly rent. Both bills will come from the electric company, but the gas bill will be itemized separately.

Most of the country has 110-120 volt current, 60 cycles, A.C. A few older houses and areas are still wired for D.C. Unless your own small appliances are geared for U.S. current or have been converted, you are well advised to leave them home. For small items, transformers can be a nuisance, although they work well for major appliances such as refrigerators or stoves. However, you can buy all kinds of appliances here at reasonable prices.

In most cities there is no charge for water, but outside city limits it may be metered, in which case you pay either monthly or quarterly. Water rates are low.

You can drink water safely from taps anywhere in the United States. Do NOT drink from brooks, wells, streams, or rivers, however. Pollution is, alas, widespread.

Tap water may taste unpleasant because it contains a high percentage of purifying chemicals. If you find this obnoxious, you can buy bottled water in the supermarket.

MOVING YOUR BELONGINGS

If you are going into a furnished apartment or house, moving is a relatively simple matter. You move exactly as you would for a stay in a hotel, though you might bring a few extra items as indicated above.

If you are moving all your household goods to this country, you or your company will probably have arranged the transfer through a specialist. Large national and international movers have experienced packers and good equipment. You should "inventory" all your belongings carefully, making separate lists of 1) those items which are going into storage, 2) those going to your new home, and 3) those going to be given away or cared for in some other way. (There is always this third category!)

Inventories should be reasonably detailed, but you can group together and record the number of boxes of "Kitchen utensils," "children's clothing," "desk contents," etc. You do not have to itemize down to the last spoon!

This is crucial advice: Have the items which you are leaving in storage picked up on an earlier day then the rest of you inventory.

Many people have the whole job done on the same day, mistakenly thinking that this is easier. It is *not!* More than one family will tell a horrendous story of having arrived at their final destination and waited weeks for their furnishings only to discover that, through some unaccountable error, the movers had confused the loads. Facing them were the goods for storage while all that they really needed was now left far behind!

Before any packers come, you should sort out the two categories into separate groupings as much as you can. Mark storage goods with a colored tag or sticker to make the difference as visible as possible. Then still carefully supervise the movers as they work.

As the boxes are being packed for your new destination, mark each completed carton clearly in large letters on the outside: "books"—"children's toys"—"kitchen supplies." This will help both the movers and you when you finally get into your new home.

When your belongings do arrive, you must be present to receive the goods. As the movers unpack, check to see that each item has arrived in good condition. The man in charge of the moving crew should make a written note of any damage *before you sign the bill.* Once you sign it, he will make no further changes. If some goods are damaged, immediately obtain a claim form from the moving company (or their insurance agent). Fill it out, *have a Xerox copy made of it for yourself,* then return the original promptly. Time is important. Don't delay. Let your own company know what has happened too so that their transportation specialist can advise you. If you are not reimbursed within two or three weeks, let the transportation officer of your firm follow-up on your claim, or do it yourself. Don't let too much time go by.

Photocopies should always be made of whatever papers or letters or claims or counterclaims pass between you and the movers and/or the insurance company. This is very important. If your company does not make the copies for you, take each paper to a public copying machine. You will find them in stationers' shops, libraries, railroad stations, and even Woolworth stores! They are simple to operate and cost only a few cents.

Having the full story in detail and in the proper sequence in your files makes following up on any claim far easier and quicker.

At no stage in the moving process should you yourself touch *anything* once the movers have arrived. Let them do *all* the packing and moving, with no exceptions. This is very important because otherwise you may cancel out all their insurance coverage. If you have touched *nothing,* then nothing can be your fault. Otherwise, everything can!

It is well to check carefully with your company some days before the movers are to arrive so that you know exactly what services you can expect. These vary according to the contract. Some will place your furniture, set up beds, and unpack china, silver, glassware, linens, and books. They are supposed to remove all packing debris. Some movers will connect your electrical appliances for you; most will not. Some will only set up large items and will not unpack small ones. Arrangements vary widely so you need to find out ahead of time which ones will apply to you. Be sure to *ask* in advance.

It is not necessary to tip the moving crew, but most people do so in relation to the size and length of the job. Tips range from $1 a man for a small job up to about $5 per man for a full day's job. It is also a good idea to have beer and coffee available if possible. This is a hard and tiring job. Be friendly with the movers, but try to stay out of their way. Time is money for them and also for you.

Chapter 16

The Most for Your Money

One newcomer to the United States, when asked his first impression, replied: "So many things to buy." And so there are!

MATERIALISM

You will find yourself being urged from every page of every newspaper and on every TV wavelength to buy all manner of goods which, in fact, you are quite happy without! This constant barrage of advertising, with its emphasis on owning this or that in order to be happy, healthy, or more attractive, has given America the reputation of being dreadfully materialistic. It is true; this is an affluent and, therefore, materialistic nation. But it is interesting to note that as soon as *any* country grows in affluence, it tends to grow more and more materialistic. Traffic jams develop in country after country as more people are able to buy cars; salesmen work harder and harder in most of the free world to sell televisions, watches, new furniture, new foods, new clothes, transistor radios, or labor-saving machines such as computers, tractors, or washing machines.

One must assume that humans everywhere are alike in this respect. As soon as there is any extra money, they seek to raise and *keep on raising* their standard of living. One need not be shocked at this, but should look at the deeper level: What do people then do with their new leisure? How much do they share it? How creative are they? How hard do they work?

Because so much in the U.S. is mass produced, there is a large quantity of goods available relatively inexpensively for everyone. You will find a tremendous range in price, variations based on quality, style, areas of the country, and other factors. Comparative price shopping is a good idea before one starts to buy any major items. This can be misleading to a newcomer. An eighteen-year-old stenographer on her first job can afford snappy-looking clothes, a TV, a shared apartment, a winter cruise (on the installment plan). This is startling to those who come from countries where such luxuries are attainable only by the rich. This young woman pays less and gets shoddier goods than her older colleague who can afford better quality—but the quick effect on the onlooker has been made, and the girl herself feels sophisticated. Almost surely she will shift upward in quality as she both earns and learns more. This is how our mobile social structure works.

From all of America's abundance, how are you, the new arrival, going to know how to get your money's worth? In the first place, don't hurry. Take time; look over the various kinds of stores and examine the quality of their merchandise; read the ads carefully so that you can compare prices; touch, explore, and examine before you buy.

In addition, there are some helpful guidelines.

FOOD

Supermarkets in someone else's country are always confusing. How can you decide what to buy amid such profusion?

Grades and Prices

You can save a good deal of money if you buy according to *grade* instead of "brand" (which only means company name).

For example, one can of beans may cost 31 cents, another, 26 cents. The more expensive one may be the *brand* that is most widely advertised and therefore best known. Perhaps you are only paying your share of the advertising costs. It is quite possible that if you buy the cheaper can, you will *not* be sacrificing quality, yet you will save several cents on just one small item.

Look to see if both cans contain the same number of ounces; look at the list of ingredients to see what percentage is water. By law actual ingredients must always be listed. The important thing to know is that the listing must be *in order of the amount contained*. So if the ingredients read: "water, macaroni, cheese," you put the package back on the shelf for you know it contains more water than macaroni.

Watch out for such words as "moisture"—which means nothing more nor less than "water"—or "salad dressing" as distinct from "mayonnaise." The law says that mayonnaise must contain 65 percent oil. So some companies put out "salad dressing," which only has to contain 30 percent oil. Some people prefer less oil, but it is good to know what you are getting so you can judge the price accordingly.

The thing that is confusing but important to understand is that our grading system (the words "Choice" or "Good" on meat, for example, or "Grade A" or "Grade B" on eggs) has *nothing* to do with the *nutritional* value of the food. All will be fresh, healthy, and nutritious. The difference in grade has to do only with *appearance*—more uniform size, whole and not in pieces, better color, less water. Let us take canned mushrooms as an example: Grades (and therefore prices) will vary depending on whether the mushrooms are whole, sliced, or in broken pieces. But *all will be good, healthy mushrooms.*

Or tomatoes: Do you need firm, uniform-sized tomatoes for a salad, for instance (Grade A), or are you going to serve them in a stew or sauce? If so, broken pieces of various sizes would be perfectly all right for your purpose (Grades B or C).

In short, when speaking of canned goods:

Grade A—Means whole, beautiful, free from defects;
Grade B—Means large pieces, but not necessarily whole;
Grade C—Means smaller and broken pieces, often lots of juice; satisfactory for cooking, but not for appearance.

The price of Grade C may be half the price of Grade A!
Much citizen pressure is being put on the U.S. government to

regulate and grade foods. As yet the grading system is not compulsory, so one does not find grades on everything. However, the U.S. Department of Agriculture is marking more and more items. It is a good idea to look for their stamp and use it whenever possible.

For example: one market offered three brands of orange juice. Prices were: 47 cents, 49 cents, and 53 cents. All three brands had a small shield printed on the can with the words "U.S. Grade A"; all three contained the same number of ounces. This meant that all three brands met the same government standards of quality. The difference in price therefore was a matter of packaging, advertising, or transportation costs. It was *not* the quality of the juice. So you can save by learning to read labels.

This same sort of price variation appears also on cigarettes, camera film, and many other common items. If in doubt, ask your friends, neighbors, and colleagues for their recommendations. (See Appendix, Part II for a list of government food grades and symbols.)

Warnings

Although an increasing effort is being made to protect the buyer, there are still, unfortunately, a number of "shortcuts" or "hidden" factors that one needs to watch out for.

Sizes and weights, for example. A bottle that looks like a quart (or liter) does not necessarily contain that amount. In tiny print on the label, it may say "Contains 24 fluid ounces." (A quart is 32.) Packages meant to look like one pound may actually contain only 14 or 11 or 9 ounces worth of food. By law, weights are printed on all food packages, under "Net Contents," so one can always look and see—but too many of us do not take the time and trouble. Often the print is very small—on purpose!

Don't be overly concerned about all these matters. You will gradually learn by experience and by trial and error, but you can shorten your learning time if you read labels and compare as you shop. You will soon find the foods your family likes and will learn which brands are best for you. Such care and study can save you a considerable amount on your food bills. The Department of Agriculture says that those who watch carefully and who follow the "weekly specials" offered in all supermarkets can save in the neighborhood of 6 percent per week.

Any large bookstore will have a selection of books helpful as guides to shopping.

CLOTHES AND FABRICS

To judge the weave, quality, weight, and texture of cloth, each person has to feel it and decide for herself. But labels are sewn into clothes too to help you know the content of the fabric—if you stop to read them! There are also labels with directions for cleaning the garment.

Suppose you buy a blouse advertised as a Dacron (drip-dry) blouse. How do you know what it is really made of? By law it *must* have a label attached telling the percentage of every kind of fiber used in the material.

Perhaps the label says: "cotton 30%, rayon 30%, Dacron 40%;" perhaps it will say "100% Dacron;" or it might include only 8% Dacron. But it could still be advertised as a "Dacron blouse."

Many people never look at labels, but if you do, you will know what you are actually getting—which might make a difference as to whether or not you want to buy it at a given price.

Buying Woolen Goods

The law states that the label must tell how much is new wool—which is called simply "wool;" how much is reused or reprocessed wool; and how much is other fibers—such as cotton or rayon.

Generally speaking, the more new wool, the better—but not always. You must feel it and judge for yourself. Sometimes a mixture of good quality new wool (at least *half*) might be better than a 100 percent wool garment, if the quality of new wool was poor in the first place.

RETURNING MERCHANDISE

If you have bought something and want to return it, you can do so with most items from nearly all department stores and often—but not always—from smaller shops. However, you must follow two rules or they will not accept the returned item:

1) The return must be made *within 10 days* of purchase;
2) You *must* have the sales slip with it.

So do not throw away any receipts, however thin and skimpy they may look, until you are sure you are satisfied with the item.

If you are returning a gift and therefore have no sales receipt, take off the delivery label from the front of the package. It has various little notes and marks on it that have meaning for the clerk. If you have no label, then ask to "exchange" for some item of equal worth. It is often easier to do this than to get a cash refund.

GUARANTEES

When you buy new electric appliances, radios, TV's, or other major items such as stoves, you will probably be given a sheaf of papers with them. One of these is likely to be a written guarantee. This means that if anything goes wrong, you can have the item repaired free of charge for a certain length of time—on some items as long as three to five years. You should read the guarantee carefully. It probably asks you to send in a postcard to establish the date of purchase. If so, be *sure* to do it. In addition, write the date of purchase on the guarantee itself along with the guarantee number. Keep it somewhere safe so you can find it if you need it. The guarantee will be of help *only* if you have saved the papers and complied with the instructions.

REPAIRS

If you have problems with vacuum cleaners, toasters, radios, and so on, look under "Electric Appliances—Repairs" or "Radio (Vacuum cleaner, etc.) Repair" in the classified section of the telephone book. Try to find a repair shop specializing in your particular brand name, if possible. Other kinds of repairs—china, glass, zippers, etc. —are also listed by item in most phone books.

TELEPHONE SALES

If anyone tries to sell you an item over the telephone, just say "No, thank you" and hang up without any further conversation. Dancing lessons, stocks, light bulbs, magazines—all sorts of things may be offered. *Don't get involved!* They will try to tempt you with every kind of prize, free demonstration, or gift. *Don't fall for it.* Reputable firms rarely use this technique for selling—any more than they use door-to-door salesmen. Newcomers to the United States should take *no chances* with telephone salesmen. It is dangerous to do so.

INSTALLMENT PLANS

Generally speaking, *avoid* installment plan buying. Costs of carrying and amortization are high and often so confusing that they are virtually hidden. Once you have signed the agreement, you are stuck with all the payments; there is no way out. So tread carefully. Mortgages on real estate, well-handled financing on the price of a car, or similar loans on very large purchases may be necessary, but try to avoid burdening yourself with monthly payments on such luxury items as washers, TV's, hi-fi's, or tempting trips to sunny beaches in the Caribbean! You often pay one third or one half as much again as the regular price by the time all fees have been figured.

BUYING WHERE IT COSTS LESS

Americans do not usually "bargain" over prices, as is familiar in much of the world. What they do instead is shop around to find the store which offers the item and quality they want at the lowest price. Almost everything sold in the United States varies in price according to the store and often the time of year (just before Christmas is often highest; lowest is just after Christmas or during August sales). Sometimes the price varies according to state or local taxes. Many people cross state lines to buy liquor, cigarettes, or automobiles, for example, because there are wide fluctuations in taxes on such items from state to state.

Discount Houses

If it is important to you to save money, look for the discount houses in your city. They exist all across the country and are of course growing in popularity in these days of inflation. Much of what they sell is comparable to goods sold elsewhere, but they can offer lower prices for any one or all of these reasons: perhaps the store offers no credit terms—therefore it saves on that operation; it may remain open for longer hours; there may be fewer sales people and less service; usually there is no delivery service except for heavy items like refrigerators; floor space is often so fully used that the store is congested; the decor is simple or non-existent so as to save the cost of fancy carpeting or expensive interiors; dressing rooms, where you try clothes on, may be communal.

In most discount houses you will find clothes hanging on long racks. Shoes may even be piled up in "bins." Your best buys in these places are apt to be such items as drugs and cosmetics, photographic equipment, housewares, bedding, small appliances, garden equipment, carpets and rugs, luggage, books and records, furniture or large household appliances. It is advisable to look for those which carry familiar brand names as much as possible, or ask a neighbor or friend to go with you.

Many of these are the very same items that you would buy in other stores at higher prices. Never look in discount stores for top-quality clothes or exclusive fashions or choice furniture. Look for goods where serviceability is more important than style (pots and pans, blue jeans, garden hoses, and so on).

Another popular American institution is the so-called dime store. No longer selling much for a dime, these stores originated in the nineteenth century when Mr. Woolworth decided that a small profit on a great volume would add up to more than a large profit on fewer sales. So he opened a chain of stores selling an enormous range of items for (in those days) 5¢ and 10¢—nothing higher. These prices have long since gone, but the various chains which have followed Woolworth's (Grant's, Kresge's, K-Mart, Lamston's, Murphy's, Green's) still carry an extraordinary variety of inexpensive items. Because they are so colorful and give such a good idea of what is available, these various "Five and Ten" stores are often of interest to newcomers who find that wandering through them also helps them to learn American names for unfamiliar items.

Buying Secondhand

So many people are constantly on the move in the United States that it is easy to find secondhand household goods for sale. Buying secondhand is quite usual here. Many young couples furnish new homes this way. People who do not want to spend time shopping sometimes buy the entire contents of an apartment from someone who is moving to another part of the country.

If you look in the local newspaper, you will see advertisements in the classified section that read:

"Moving, entire contents of house for sale."
"Going to California. Have desk, large clock, child's bicycle for sale."
"Redecorated house. Complete living room furniture for sale—Louis XIV style."

If you see something that interests you, call *at once* on the telephone; such things are often sold very quickly. If it is still available, go immediately to examine it. If you like an item, you can try bargaining. Then you must work out a means of getting the goods to your house. This can be a major problem, but the easiest solution (if you have no friend with a van) is to look at ads in the local paper or in the Classified Directory under "Trucking" to find a man with a truck. If you have a car or if you are going to move goods a long distance, it is cheaper to rent a "U-Haul" truck or trailer (to attach to your car). Give a deposit to hold the goods and *get a receipt*. Don't pay the full price until you come back with the truck to pick up the items. Most people are honest and are dealing in a straight-forward manner, but there can be "rackets"—so you need to be a little wary.

A very popular practice is for people to collect all the items they no longer need such as furniture, glassware, china, etc. They price them and have a one or two day sale in their garage. Sometimes several families or even an entire neighborhood will hold a cooperative sale. "Garage Sales" or "Tag" sales are advertised in local newspapers and by signs on the streets near the sale site. Good bargains can often be found and talking with the owners and other customers is fun.

Buying in this way is a good deal more trouble than buying new equipment from a store and having it delivered, but it can also be much cheaper. Many times, you get real bargains and very high quality, especially if the owner must move and is in a hurry to dispose of his goods or if someone has died and an estate is being settled.

Thrift Shops

Thrift shops are run by charities which first collect and then sell used clothes, bric-a-brac, sports equipment, books, china, glass-ware, and so on. The charities then donate the money they collect to some particular school, hospital, old people's home, or other institution.

There is no loss of face in buying at such shops. Many of the wealthiest society people donate to them, help to run them, and also buy from them. They are particularly good for such items as children's clothes (often outgrown before they were much used) or evening dresses which the well-to-do "donate" after a few wearings, but which most of us wear so seldom that we want to buy at minimum cost! Many people go to thrift shops for fur coats, ice skates, tennis rackets, books, or for pictures, lamps, or "extras" of that sort for their new homes. By law all clothing given to reputable shops has been dry-cleaned and inspected so you need have no worries about that if you select a well-run charity shop.

Chapter 17

Household Help and Baby-Sitters

Domestic help is so expensive nowadays that most Americans do their own housework. The only common exceptions are:

1) Cleaning women who come in once or twice a week;
2) Baby-sitters who stay with children when the parents go out.

For the rest, precooked and packaged foods, disposable or no-iron fabrics, dishwashers and washing machines, laundromats and coin-operated dry cleaners—all such time and labor-saving devices—take the place of household help.

TO FIND A CLEANING WOMAN

The best way is by word of mouth. Start with your friends or the wives of your husband's business acquaintances. This is a normal request, and you need not feel embarrassed. Americans are accustomed to helping each other find domestic help as it is difficult to do so. People will ask their own help if they have extra time to give, or a relative or a friend to suggest.

Ask the superintendent of your apartment house. Perhaps there is someone already working in the building who has extra time. This will *not* be the superintendent's daughter or sister, as would be true in much of the world, but he often knows the tenants' "help" and can ask them. If he finds someone for you, he will expect a tip—$5 or up depending on circumstances. Sometimes the clerks at local laundries, groceries, or the like can give you suggestions. If you are known to be a regular customer, such people are likely to recommend people carefully.

If you cannot find anyone by word of mouth, there are other methods—though these tend to be less satisfactory:

153

You can use a Maid Service (listed as such in the Classified Telephone Directory).

Such services are expensive, but on the other hand they look after troublesome details like Social Security payments, insurance, and so on. There are House Cleaning Services, too. They send a team of well-equipped people in to wash windows, clean rugs, and do similar heavy work at regular intervals—or once or twice a year as you request.

You can use an Employment Agency.

This is likely to be expensive and is not a preferred way. There is no guarantee that the person will stay with you beyond the period covered by the usually high agency fee.

Furthermore, you may have to interview many people. If you use this method, be *sure* to ask for references and be *sure* to consult a good agency. Not every agency is dependable either.

You can advertise.

Also not a good way, as you know nothing about the people who may come streaming into your house to be interviewed. If you do follow this method, check each reference very carefully before hiring. Don't try it unless your English is very good.

You can answer an advertisement.

People in small towns or country areas can answer local ads and usually find help; if you are in a larger town, it is also a possible method if you interview carefully and check references. Some of the best prospects are found in foreign language papers.

IF YOU NEED HELP FOR A PARTY

If you have a cleaning woman and find her efficient, you can ask if she would like to help you serve in the evening; often they are willing. Sometimes they have friends whom they recommend, or they may send their daughters.

If you would rather have trained help look under "Maid Service" in the trusty Classified Directory. You can hire waitresses, cooks, bartenders, or butlers by the hour.

If you live in a college town, call the Employment Bureau of the university. Some colleges hold extracurricular training programs in household skills or bartending to help students in getting jobs. Other students just sign up for general help and can be hired by the hour. Some are excellent helpers; others are sloppy and irresponsible. Try to interview before your party so you can judge for yourself.

BABY-SITTERS

Today only one person in five in the United States lives within 50 miles of his birthplace. Since the country was first settled, Americans have moved around a great deal, and are often far away from their parents. Because they have broken ties with their past at a young age, chosen their own occupations, established their own homes and developed their own lifestyles, few American children grow up closely surrounded by grandparents, aunts, uncles, and cousins as they do in Italy, Nigeria, or India, for example. This, along with the fact that modern American families do not have servants, has made the "baby-sitter" a vital part of the American scene. A "sitter" is someone who is hired to care for children for a specific length of time—usually relatively short—while the parents are out for an evening, going to a party or a course of study for example. Sometimes the baby-sitter is also hired for longer periods, perhaps when the parents are away for a weekend. In such cases the "sitter" is likely to be a mature and motherly woman. For short periods, teen-agers, college students, nursing students, and others (of either sex) are commonly employed on an hourly basis.

From the point of view of convenience, the best sitters are often young people who live in your apartment building or close by in the neighborhood. This gives you a chance to meet the parents and see what they are like. If an emergency occurs, young sitters can call upon their parents quickly for help; you do not have to take them far to see them home at night or pay expensive taxi fares. Another advantage is that young people living close by can usually fill in quite readily on short notice or for short periods of time.

In an apartment house you can ask the superintendent for permission to post a notice for a baby-sitter by the mailboxes. This is often the best way to find out if there is anyone in the building who is interested in baby-sitting. Retired people as well as students are often glad to earn a little money in this way and can be found by such a note.

An excellent source is the Nursing School of a hospital. The students frequently want to earn extra money in their spare time. They are already considered to be reliable or they would not have been accepted into the nursing school. The normal procedure is to get the telephone number of a dormitory and then call. Ask whoever answers if there is a willing baby-sitter around. Better yet, go to the school *before you need a sitter,* ask about the possibilities, and contact one or two students.

With any luck, you might find one or two students at a nearby college who come from your own country and speak your language. If they get to know and like you, they will come to you whenever they can.

The *disadvantage* of all students is that they are often busy in the evenings; they will not work during their holidays; and sometimes they bring along their friends. The *advantage* is that they are less expensive than anyone from an agency and, being young, are likely to be more fun for your children.

Again, if you like your cleaning woman, she herself may be willing to do some evening sitting, or may know of someone who would like to earn a little extra money.

Other sources could be the bulletin board of the local YWCA or the Girl Scouts who sometimes organize baby-sitting services. Some Scout Troops train older girls who earn service credits in this way. They are a particularly good possibility if you want someone to remain indoors and play with the children. Since they are young themselves, you might not want to give them outside responsibility, for example, taking children through traffic.

As you make friends, don't hesitate to ask if their teen-agers would like to baby-sit. Often they are delighted. This work is done by everyone—do not be shy about asking teen-agers whether or not they are available. Most mothers try to line up three or four sitters whom they (and the children) get to know and like. In this way they have alternate numbers to call in case of need.

A young couple struggling along on a tight budget—especially students—often work out an exchange agreement with another couple, "sitting" for each other's children a certain number of hours or evenings a week. The mothers exchange daytime hours as well, giving each other occasional or regular free afternoons for such things as shopping, taking a course of study, going to the hairdresser, or visiting friends.

Rates vary widely by location and age—less for teen-agers than for mature women, for example.

You pay more for daytime hours than the period after children are in bed—until midnight. After that, rates go up again. You pay more, of course, if several children are in the family and more if the job includes preparing a meal. Many "sitters" will not do that. One should not expect it.

If you have a small baby and want someone more responsible than a student, look under "Nurse Registries" or "Baby-Sitting Services" in the Classified Directory. If you employ the same person for even a few hours per month, you must pay Social Security taxes (see below) unless you get them through an agency. In that case the agency will do the paperwork for you.

CHURCH NURSERIES

Most churches have nurseries and baby-sitting services on Sunday mornings so that parents can attend services. There is usually no charge—or only a nominal one—for this service.

Many churches also run nursery schools and kindergartens during the week. Parents need not be members of the church. Some list parishioners who like to baby-sit; some have set up group baby-sitting for certain afternoons during the week so that mothers can shop or attend to other necessities. Ask also about public and private day care centers, neighborhood centers, or nursery schools.

TAXES ON HOUSEHOLD EMPLOYEES

Household employees include cooks, cleaning women, baby-sitters, handymen, drivers, gardeners.

These rules may guide you:

If you pay any household employee $50 or more in any calendar quarter (that is, three-month period, January to March, etc.), or as little as $3.50 a week, you are *required to pay* a Social Security tax on a percent of the total wages paid. This amount may be matched by the employee—or you may pay the whole amount.

Whoever pays, you, as the employer, are responsible for mailing the total amount of tax within a month after the end of each calendar quarter to your local Internal Revenue Service (IRS) office (see telephone book under U.S. Government).

The IRS will send you a quarterly reminder to pay this tax. All you need do is write to their local office and ask for "Form 942."

If you are not now paying the taxes you owe, write the IRS explaining why you have not done so and estimate the total amount of wages you have failed to report. They will then inform you as to the amount of back taxes and interest owed. Do not delay. It is better to clear the record at once, as penalties build up the longer one is overdue.

Actually, the amounts involved are not great even when you pay the full tax quarter yourself, but you can be in trouble if you do not comply with the rules.

Chapter 18

Schools in the United States

Education has been called America's religion. Today more than 56 million Americans are attending school. One half of all the people in the country between the ages of eighteen and twenty-five are enrolled in either a college or university; close to 49 million boys and girls are going to school. Education is an enormous (and expensive) part of American life. Its size is matched by its variety. The widely different educational systems and possibilities are as difficult for an outsider to understand as anything about American life.

Differences in American schools compared with those found in the majority of other countries lie in the fact that education here has long been intended for everyone—not just for a privileged elite. Schools are expected to meet the needs of every child, regardless of ability, and also the needs of society itself. This means that tax-supported public schools offer more than academic subjects. It surprises many people when they come here to find high schools offering such courses as typing, sewing, radio repair, computer programming, or driver training, along with traditional academic subjects such as mathematics, history, and languages. Students choose their curricula from a large "smorgasbord" of courses, depending on their interests, future goals, and level of ability. The underlying goal of American education is to develop every child to the utmost of his or her own possibilities, *however great or small these may be,* and to give each one a sense of civic and community consciousness.

Because there is no national religion and because there are so many different backgrounds and origins among the people, schools have traditionally played an important role in creating national unity and "Americanizing" the millions of immigrants who have poured into this country from its earliest days. Schools still play a large role in the community, especially in small towns.

The approach to teaching may seem unfamiliar to many, not only because it is informal, but also because there is less emphasis on learning *facts* than is true in the systems of many other countries. Instead, Americans try to teach their children to think for themselves, to delve, to explore, to develop their own intellectual and creative abilities. Students spend much time learning how to use resource materials, libraries, statistics, computers. Americans believe that if children are taught to *reason* well and to *research* well, they will be able to find whatever facts they need throughout the rest of their lives. Knowing how to solve problems is considered more important than the accumulation of facts.

This is America's answer to the searching question that thoughtful parents all over the world are asking themselves in this fast-moving time: "How can one prepare today's child for a tomorrow that one can neither predict nor understand?"

Naturally, when any family moves from one country to another, the question of schooling for their children is always an urgent one. Various choices will be open to you in the United States. Within or near whatever community you live in, there will be available to you a variety of schools—public, parochial or private; day or boarding; coeducational or all-boy/all-girl; traditional or experimental.

PUBLIC SCHOOLS

The great majority of American children attend public schools (that is, schools that are tax-supported and free). It is often confusing to people to find that there is no nationally directed standardized system for all the 50 states. Each state has been free to develop its own levels and plans. These vary so widely in quality, facilities, disciplines, and academic standards that people often move into (or out of) a state because of the level of available schooling.

To make matters even more confusing, local school districts have considerable leeway *within* each state framework. Local city, township, and district schools have their own patterns, boards, budgets, and standards, even though these must follow certain broad guidelines outlined by their states.

School support comes primarily from taxes at state and local levels, rather than from national funds. When the federal government does contribute to education, it does so primarily in the poorer states, where local funds are inadequate. National funds tend to be channeled for buildings, transportation, school lunch programs, or other supplements which do not affect the curriculum. As we have said above, Americans jealously guard their independence from their own national government! If there is even a chance that, as a result of accepting national funds, the government may be able to exert some kind of control, such funds are often turned down by community School Boards (elected citizens). There have been heated arguments—even riots and demonstrations at the college level—when citizens have felt that the National Government was exerting too strong an influence on some curriculum through support of scientific research programs, for example, or military training or other specific projects. Since many of our forebears and many of today's new citizens have come to this country for the express purpose of escaping too much government control, this feeling still runs deep.

In line with this emphasis on local control over education, there are no national examinations at either school or college levels as there are, for example, in France or England. College Board examinations, which are taken across the country for entrance to colleges and universities, are administered by a *private* organization, not by the Federal Government, and no college is compelled to use them. Similarly, a private organization, the National Board of Medical Examiners, administers a licensing examination for physicians. The results of these are accepted by virtually every state, although each state has its own examination system. This practice is common among other professions as well.

This state and local independence results, as was mentioned above, in substantial variation in the quality of public education even from one town to the next. In our fast-growing cities, public elementary and high schools are nearly all badly overcrowded. In recent years many have been troubled with violence, teacher strikes and other problems. In suburban areas and small towns, public schools tend to be more settled with adequate facilities, reasonable ratios between teachers and pupils, and good academic standards.

Feel free to raise questions and talk as freely as you like about schooling with any Americans you meet. Many people here are deeply concerned about the whole question of education. They constantly discuss the subject among themselves. They will be delighted to talk with you about it too. Much is good and much is bad in our current educational establishment. A great deal of change is under way; many values are being reconsidered. We are in the throes of reevaluating and restructuring the whole educational system of this country in order to meet the urgent needs of this scientific twentieth century, including many new pressures from our vast and rapidly changing population.

PAROCHIAL SCHOOLS

These are the Roman Catholic and other denominational counterparts to America's public school system. Not all communities have parochial schools, but many do. They, too, vary widely. They are supported not by taxes, but by religious denominations. There are some fees connected with attendance at a parochial school, but these are generally lower than for other private schools.

PRIVATE SCHOOLS

Private schools receive no financial support from tax funds and are—without exception—expensive. Some are more expensive than others, but all are costly and prices continue to rise rapidly.

Why do people spend so much money—often to the point of major financial sacrifice—to send their children to private schools? The reasons vary:

1) Classes tend to be smaller with greater individual attention. Some children need this kind of supportive individual instruction.

2) Most private schools are highly selective; through interviews, references, and examinations (at least for the upper levels), they seek students of quality. This means that they usually can maintain higher academic standards than the public schools which have to accept students of all abilities and carry them to the age of 16.

3) Some parents living in crowded or academically poor areas feel they must send their children to private schools if they are to be well enough prepared for admission to college.

4) A few parents prefer to send their children to schools sponsored by their own religious denominations.

5) Some parents seek a more nearly homogeneous student body than is found in the public schools.

Those interested in finding out about private schools can write ahead for preliminary advice from Advisory Service on Private Schools and Colleges, 500 Fifth Avenue, New York, N.Y. If you write from abroad, be sure to enclose an international money order to cover return postage. If you will be in the New York area, you are welcome to visit the office after you arrive in the United States, but you can get much initial advice by mail.

In your letter include details about the kind of school in which you are interested (for example: "a boys' school in or near such-and-such a city, strong on academic preparation with the emphasis on languages" or "a small coeducational boarding school in the country for a shy fourteen-year-old girl who stutters").

Include an indication of your price range if possible, ask about scholarship possibilities, mention whether or not you prefer a church-affiliated school, indicate your preference for day or boarding, and tell how far away from your base city would be acceptable. Send along a copy of your child's school record—that is, a list of the courses taken with the grades received.

Each private school has its own admissions procedures—most of them are difficult to get into, many have long waiting lists. Once you know the names of some suitable schools, write for their catalogues. Then follow their instructions regarding application for enrollment.

BOARDING SCHOOLS

These exist mostly for children of high school age, though there are a few for younger children too. If you happen to settle near a boarding school, you may be able to enroll your child as a day student.

NURSERY SCHOOLS

There is such variation in preschools that it is best to wait until you arrive to see what is available in your neighborhood. Private nursery schools are often expensive, but there are also informal play groups, church-affiliated nursery schools, morning programs at local YWCA's, or other less expensive possibilities in most communities.

Little children normally attend these for only two or three hours, once or twice a week, but they start to learn about sharing, following instructions, and being part of a group, and they enjoy the companionship of other children their age, which is often hard to find in city living.

If you live in a housing area where there are many small children and an outdoor place to play, you probably will not need such an organized group. However, in an impersonal concrete-and-glass apartment-house world, children are sometimes lonely. In addition, parents coming from abroad like to give their children a little extra help in learning English and American ways before they start in the "rough and tumble" of a real school.

If you do not find a preschool that you like near your home, you may find that there are dance classes, painting sessions, swimming lessons, or other activities for little children through which you can bring your child into contact with playmates once or twice a week.

Large apartment units often provide day care or supervised play groups for little children during certain hours of the week. Mothers sometimes pool their resources and take turns with each other's children in the playground, partly to give themselves an occasional free afternoon, and partly to give their children needed companionship.

When you are settled in your new area, you will be able to explore the possibilities near your home.

RELATIONSHIPS BETWEEN PARENT AND SCHOOL

The degree to which American parents are involved in their children's schools is often surprising to people of other countries. Most schools have organizations made up of both parents and teachers (usually called P.T.A. from the initials of the "Parent-Teacher Association"). They meet together regularly to discuss and confer on various matters pertaining to the school—curriculum, budgets, faculty, salaries, library facilities, or whatever it may be.

Mothers often volunteer to help with classroom or after-school activities. They sometimes make costumes for plays or play the piano or assist a teacher on a class field trip. Some of them give regular time, under the teacher's supervision, in working with tutoring children in the classroom.

In good schools a real effort is made to have both the home and the school work together for the child's well-being. You will generally find teachers eager to talk with you about any problems you may have concerning your child—although the larger the school (understandably), the less likely this is to happen. Where size permits, there are often parent conferences, scheduled appointments so that parents can meet privately with one or more of their child's teachers to discuss his particular problems or progress. You will be sent notices of meetings or programs to which you are invited. Do try to go to as many as you can.

Both mothers and fathers are expected to attend such meetings and to show their interest in the school. You may be invited to a "Parents' Day," where you follow a child's schedule through a full day of classes. This is enlightening and enjoyable for most parents.

School activities provide a good way to meet your neighbors and to make friends in the community. Since Americans enjoy meeting people from other countries, you will probably find your national background a help rather than a handicap in getting acquainted. This is true even if you are having trouble with the language.

AFTER-SCHOOL OR "EXTRACURRICULAR" ACTIVITIES

In addition to their academic work, children in the United States are offered a wide range of activities in the after-school hours.

These are designed to help broaden their skills, abilities and appreciation of life; to give them a chance to practice leadership and assume responsibilities; to supplement school courses; and to provide additional outlets and stimuli. There is often a range of activities from which to choose, such as nature clubs, musical organizations, science clubs, art and drama groups, or language clubs. A wide selection of sport activities is always available. Virtually every school has a student-run newspaper; often a photographic darkroom is also available. Some of these activities take place during the school day, but many are held after classes are over. Even though they are optional, they are considered a part of the American educational experience. Parents encourage their children to participate in those programs that best suit their own special talents and interests. Much is learned during these off-duty hours, especially in terms of human "give-and-take." Americans believe this includes human relationships, social skills, and a well-trained body, as well as intellectual development. Both employers and college admissions officers in the United States carefully consider the extracurricular activities in which students have participated, both during their free time after school and also during the long holidays. These indicate to them something of a young person's leadership potential, enthusiasm, creativity, breadth of interest, vitality and personality. They weigh these qualities, together with the academic record, in order to assess a student's intelligence, perseverance, and ability to *use* what he knows, rather than merely repeating it by rote on examination papers.

THE SCHOOL YEAR

For most schools the term begins in early September and ends somewhere near the middle or end of June. A few schools, generally at the high school level, also offer summer sessions. These are optional, but they give students a chance to make up work that they have missed or failed, take advance credits or extra courses they have not had time for in the school year, or just become familiar with a school before the new term starts.

Summer sessions normally hold classes in the morning, then offer a range of sports, trips, and leisure activities in the afternoon.

If you arrive in the United States in the spring with a teen-ager who plans to enter a regular school session in September, you might want to consider enrolling him or her in summer courses to improve English language proficiency, help them make friends, gain self-confidence, or perhaps just get out of a hot city!

Most American school systems are structured as follows:

Elementary school runs from kindergarten or the first grade to the sixth grade (ages five or six to welve years);

Junior high usually consists of grades seven and eight (ages thirteen and fourteen), although sometimes ninth grade is also included;

High school normally consists of grades nine through twelve (ages fifteen to eighteen).

School is compulsory from the ages of six to sixteen throughout the nation.

THE DESEGREGATION OF SCHOOLS

"We are a long way from being home free," says Mr. William White, Education Specialist for the U.S. Commission on Civil Rights, referring to the desegregation of schools in the United States. Progress in providing equal access to educational opportunity for both Black and White children in the U.S. has been made since the Supreme Count banned so-called "separate but equal" public schools in 1954, but it has been very slow, particularly in large cities, in both south and north. Surprisingly perhaps, the south, where the prior situation was worse, led in desegregation moves at first. Now, however, "resegregation" has started to take place in a number of communities where White people, taking their children out for private schooling, are leaving many public schools essentially Black again.

Efforts have been made to try to assure that more or less equal numbers of Black and White children attend school together. Because housing is also often segregated to varying degrees, however, this has required elaborate systems of transporting children (both Black and White) to schools which are often quite far from their homes. Parents of both groups often object strongly.

Those coming to the States will read and hear a good deal about this issue of "bussing" in many parts of the country. It is an emotional subject. In some cases it has caused racial violence; in other communities the system has worked peacefully and well. Some urban areas, where the problems remain acute, are now trying a new method of combining quadrants of their own cities (administratively) with parts of neighboring suburbs, trying to create a more balanced mixture of children without the need for long bus trips.

Although progress has been slow and all kinds of delaying tactics are still often used by dissenters, most education experts consider that there have been heartening and substantial gains, even though incomplete and geographically spotty. Advances are evidenced by the fact that not only Blacks but all minorities are going to colleges in far greater numbers—to better colleges, and to professional and graduate schools.

In the long run, of course, access to equal education is the only road to real job equality in the land. Most major cities still have a long way to go at both elementary and secondary levels. Much remains to be done in desegregating both schools and housing. However, the nation is struggling to make progress in both areas.

SUMMER CAMPS AND JOBS

Camps

Partly because of summer heat but mostly because we began as an agricultural nation, summer holidays are very long. Children and youth get restless if they are idle for too long, especially when they are living in cramped city apartments. As a result there are thousands of different kinds of summer camps for children. They are run by many organizations such as Boy and Girl Scouts, YM or YWCA, or churches. There are also many private camps which, although expensive, provide horseback riding, skilled instruction in various specialties, wilderness trips, and the like, which the cheaper camps cannot do.

Older teen-agers are more likely to seek summer jobs or go off with their own age groups on camping or other trips. Many go back-packing in the mountains of the West. Anyone living in a city apartment may want to encourage such summer prospects for their young people.

Jobs

Many teen-agers earn a good portion of their college expenses by working during the summer at such jobs as waiting tables, deck hand, harvester, construction worker, camp counselor, mother's helper, gas station attendant, or telephone operator or messenger. They are not concerned with status. Being unskilled, they try to find jobs at whatever level they can. They seek not only money, but also experience. They learn work habits, responsibility, the ability to take orders and to get along with a boss and new kinds of people. As they grow older and more competent, most of them get better jobs, probably still unskilled but more closely tied to their fields of interest—in hospitals, political headquarters, newspapers, schools, or wherever. Students from abroad should check carefully into visa regulations if they also want to use the long holidays in this way. The Dean or Foreign Student Advisor at any school or college should be able to offer advice here, but the visa question should be raised in one's home country before leaving.

Chapter 19

Teen-age Dating

The affluence, independence, and social freedom of American youth are frightening to many visiting parents as they contemplate bringing young people into America's teen-age world.

One of the most difficult things to accept is the fact that to a large degree youth in America sets its own rules, regulations, and patterns—parents here have less to say than in most countries about their children's actions outside the home, especially after the magic age of sixteen (the age of a driving license and often a car!). This independence is shattering to many parents from abroad who react by "forbidding" their children to take part in American teen-age activities, insisting instead that they come home directly from school and not go on evening "dates." These dates normally include attending movies, school dances, and parties at other people's houses, and eating out in public places.

It is difficult for a young person to be so excluded because in the United States there are no alternatives. Virtually everyone of their age group dates in one way or another. This is the way the transition is made here from parent-dominated family life to marriage. It covers a long span.

There are certain things many American parents do insist upon: 1) Some set curfew hours according to the youth's age, insisting on their return at the appointed hour; 2) Boys are expected to be responsible and usually take the girl home; 3) Parents can expect a boy to call at the front door rather than just honking his car's horn from the curb.

From eight or nine years old upward, while children are still interested in members of their own sex, they love to visit overnight in each other's houses. Children, especially girls, have "Pajama

Parties'' or "Sleep Overs.'' This merely means that they like to spend the night together in one of their houses under parental supervision. There is much giggling, whispering, possibly some candy-making, pillow-fighting, and so on. It is noisy but harmless, and part of the growing-up process. In summer boys may want to sleep outdoors in a pup tent or tree house or on a "Camp-Out." To children of these ages, sleeping away from home marks the first stages of independence; they like to do it in groups.

The next stage is an interest in the opposite sex—first, mostly talk and giggle, then, long before they are ready emotionally or financially to marry, they start "dating."

This does not necessarily mean that they indulge in sex, despite reports to the contrary. Many of them do not, despite youth's widespread questioning of previous social patterns. Premarital chastity is no longer considered the major virtue it once was, but despite considerable "petting," caressing, and fondling, young people are not necessarily as "loose" sexually as many adults assume.

Some parents from abroad may find more difficult to accept the freer attitude towards racial, religious and class distinctions among American youth at the dating age. This and the freer, more independent and often more aggressive role of girls in America may prove to be difficult adjustments at first for many teen-agers and parents accustomed to other cultural patterns.

It is interesting to note that youth generally sets, and also obeys, its own rules. These rules vary by locality and age group, but the young do set their own standards to a large degree. Some groups are quite strict within their own codes, others more relaxed. Young people also set their own forms of dress and speech, and those within each group conform. Fashions vary by locality, and to some extent also by economic level and social background; fads come and go within a group, but everyone shifts at the same time and anyone who does not may be considered strange. The penalty for not conforming to their own rules is likely to be loss of reputation, loss of popularity, or both.

At any large school students are likely to be able to choose from among various kinds of groups, ranging all the way from what the young call "straight" (that is conformist conservative) to long-haired, poorly-dressed "freaks." (Names and descriptions will probably change even before this book is published, but the range of difference will remain constant.) Although strong conformity is usual *within* each group, a young person is free to choose which kind of group he or she prefers to join.

DATING

There are various types of teen-age dating. The one in vogue in your community will depend on the part of the country, current local fads, and somewhat on age levels.

Casual Dating

It is quite possible to go to a dance with one person, a football game with another, and a picnic with a third. Sometimes two couples go out together. This is known as "double-dating".

"Going With"

Often, however, young people pair up with just one partner. They do everything together—going with one another to all the parties; making constant telephone calls to each other; exchanging rings, bracelets, sweaters and so on;—in short, being totally wrapped up in each other. (Girls tend to be more "serious" about these relationships than boys.) This relationship can last anywhere from a week to several years. At the high school level it rarely leads to marriage although sex can be expected and a break-up can be quite emotional.

Group Dating

Large groups of girls and boys may also go around together. There can be almost constant physical contact such as handholding or arms draped around each other, which often distresses parents. In many groups, however, the youths are extremely strict in their codes of behavior. Some are religiously oriented.

In accord with the general trend toward equality between the sexes, more and more girls pay some or part of their way on dates, especially if they have as much money as the boy. This is often called "going Dutch Treat." Since girls are becoming more aggressive, it is quite common nowadays for them to initiate a date . . . don't be surprised if a girl calls your son!

Some American parents help their children in every way they can from an early age to be popular with the opposite sex. It is felt that through mixing easily with other young people, teen-agers gain self-assurance and experience in human relationships. The United States is a group-oriented society and there is concern when people prefer solitude. American parents may worry if they think their child is a "loner," feeling it is important for their children to have many friends. However, the young person who prefers to read, or play the violin, or be alone, is quite free to do so, and will also be respected by those around him or her.

A growing concern in some quarters is the increase in acceptance of "gay" and "lesbian" attachments. These preferences are rarely expressed by people before their early twenties and the greatest difficulty for parents seems to be that they may have inadvertently caused homosexual tendencies in their children.

Many middle-class American youth are very affluent. Many earn their spending money themselves. Teen-agers often have cars, which is jarring to some foreign visitors. It is not necessarily merely luxurious living, however. Distances in this country are great, and public transportation is often limited, especially outside major cities. Teen-agers often need cars to get to jobs, attend classes, or meet their friends.

The great majority of young people are responsible, hard-working and steady, despite overseas news stories to the contrary. Unfortunately some—especially in or near big cities—are spoiled and irresponsible or are apathetic or disillusioned about life. "What's in it for me?" is a common attitude. Drug usage is still widespread though by no means universal among youth. Alcohol is also widely used now, even among 12-14 year olds in some areas.

Parents are advised to talk quite openly with school counselors and other parents about the situation in a given school, before enrollment if possible. They are deeply concerned too. Most will talk with you honestly about it if you ask. They may not bring the subject up if you do not.

Many of the problems of youth result from the social changes that are being experienced in this country: high divorce rates, insecurity, shifts of population, breakdown of moral and sex codes, and the picture of this on television all have a strong impact on the young.

The more one's children spend time with stable families who are church-oriented, or have jobs, or are otherwise active in solid community affairs, the less likely they are to find themselves among disillusioned or irresponsible groups of young people. But today parents cannot "assume" that all is well. They must be alert to what is going on in the school, in the neighborhood, and among their children's companions.

Despite worries over teen-age morality in this open society, parents will find much that is good in the system too. The depth and freedom of discussion, the vitality and initiative, a deep sense of public and community service among many, the easy camaraderie of American youth, can provide great experiences for young visitors. The newcomers will inevitably take part in life with their school friends. One should not try to prevent it. If they are made to seem "queer" or "different" by parental decree, they may become very lonely, for they will be cut off by their schoolmates.

Parents can exert an *indirect* influence, however. First, of course, they have the all-important choice of neighborhood and school. In addition they can encourage, in an inconspicuous way, certain of their children's friendships more than others. They can provide outside activities with different young people—ski trips, for example, or volunteer projects, or a photography class, or summer excursions. Parents should get to know their child's school and other parents; join the Parent-Teacher group; attend all school functions; offer their services on school committees. The more you take part in the school life, the more you will understand your child and his/her friends.

One should not come to America worried about one's children. The overwhelming majority of American young people are serious-minded and clean-spirited. However, undeniably, in this troubled world, youth is restless everywhere. Problems do arise. Since American parents as well as visitors are naturally concerned about any difficulties their children may be experiencing, there are many sources of advice and guidance in this country, all of which are freely available to any parent. If you are concerned, you will be able to ask advice. Nearly all schools, for example, have counselors. It is the job of these men or women to advise either students or parents who are perplexed or insecure in any way. It might be wise for you and your children to go together to talk with your school's counselor soon after your arrival, well *before* there are any problems. Ask the counselor about the local dating situation, school activities, all the various possibilities and patterns in both the community and school. Then you can *plan* your choices instead of just finding your way by chance.

Ministers, priests, or rabbis are also available to advise those who wish to consult them.

Most public libraries have "young adult" sections. Librarians will help you to find useful information along these lines if you ask their aid. As in every other phase of adjusting to this new culture, you should feel free to ask those around you for their ideas and advice. Parents are everywhere; you will find them interested in your thoughts, your problems, and your reactions to the whole picture of teen-age youth. They will not be embarrassed to discuss the subject, and you need feel no hesitation either.

Chapter 20

Religion — In and Out of Church

In large cities it is possible to find places of worship for most of the major faiths, including Moslem mosques and Hindu or Buddhist temples. This reflects again the variety of people from all over the world who now make their homes in the United States. However, rather understandably, in smaller towns or rural areas, you will in all probability find only Christian churches (of several denominations) and Jewish synagogues.

Especially in small towns, churches are centers for much social and community life. Here you will find such activities as church suppers, dances, discussion groups, sports and social get-togethers, youth programs, and the like. Although you will not be given a personal invitation to these events, you will be welcome at any of them; they are held for the express purpose of including everyone in the life of the church. Church groups welcome you, regardless of your faith.

If you do not see a church of your own faith near your new home, turn to the Classified Directory under "Churches." If you find a church you like and want to attend regularly, just introduce yourself to the minister. If you make the first move, you will find yourself welcomed, helped to meet people, and assisted in many ways to "settle into" the community.

Our churches offer so much in the way of social life that some people find it overwhelming. No one need take part in any more than he or she wants to. People may urge you, in the desire to make you feel welcome. But if you prefer to participate only in the worship services, do not feel that you are obligated to do more. It is a completely personal choice. The types of activities you will find most churches offer in addition to the services include nursery

177

178   **Living in the U.S.A.**

schools for little children; after-school programs for older ones; lunches, discussion groups, or voluntary work opportunities; outings or breakfasts; concerts and plays.

Many churches hold "Coffee Hours" after the Sunday morning service. These are informal and friendly. Anyone who wants to just drifts into the Parish House or social room for coffee and cake. No one waits to be invited. It is open for everyone, but everyone is then expected to talk to people, introducing themselves whether or not they know anyone. You have some refreshment, chat with anybody you see there, and leave whenever you want. It is a pleasant, easy way to meet people of the neighborhood.

Chapter 21

Finding Friends and Having Fun

THE LAND OF LEISURE TIME?

American workers keep demanding and getting shorter and shorter working hours; they are now discussing the idea of a four-day work week. Numbers of firms are in fact already trying the shorter week. Since machines have speeded up work in homes as well as factories, both men and women have more free time than ever before in our history. Because Americans play hard and rather loudly, a visitor's first impression may be one of mass holidaying —of camper-trucks rolling down the highways, crowded beaches, packed baseball stadiums, endless television. In order to understand the true picture of how Americans use their leisure, however, one needs to look below this noisy surface.

It is true of course that much leisure is used to play. It is a country of sports—hunting and fishing, swimming, sailing, and golfing are available at all prices to all levels of workers. Americans by the million love both to play and to watch team sports like baseball or football. They bowl, roller skate, ski, or follow active sports of every kind. Also, by the million, they watch television, take part in community orchestras, make their own films or recordings, go camping, travel, garden, read books, and pursue many crafts and hobbies. Being part of a "do-it-yourself" country, people enjoy building their own shelves or boats, sewing their own clothes, developing their own photographs; they do such things for fun as well as for economy.

This is a "self-improvement" country too. More than 25 million adults are enrolled in one kind of course or another, mostly on their own time, at their own expense.

179

VOLUNTEERING

In addition to the time spent on personal pursuits, Americans volunteer a tremendous amount of time for the varied needs of their communities. It has been said that "If all the volunteers of the country withdrew, the nation would come to a halt." This would include hospitals, many schools, libraries, museums, playgrounds, community centers, welfare projects, clinics, and so on.

Why do so many Americans work long, hard hours, often at dull and disagreeable work, without pay? What is their motive? Why do they do it?

There are several answers. The concept of cooperating for mutual benefit, a sense of interlocking responsibility, a willingness to work together, are all deeply rooted in American history. The original pioneer settlers *had* to work together to survive. They had crossed dangerous seas and risked all they had in their struggle for political and religious liberation. We have seen that much of that deep-seated distrust of central government remains and crops out in all aspects of American life. People still prefer to do things themselves within their communities, rather than give a government agency control or wait for its bureaucratic delays.

Sometimes volunteering results because Americans want to achieve something for which no money is paid. So they come together to contribute their energies—as is done in many lands. They may work together to put a new roof on a church, to send parcels to flood victims, to provide summer holidays for underprivileged children, or to clean up a polluted stream. People will give time after a long hard day to work on a Town Zoning Commission or School Board or Planning Committee. They care about their town.

Hundreds of thousands of so-called leisure hours go into hard, sustained, unpaid work on one or another community need. As you read the local newspapers, you will see that Americans are constantly forming new kinds of citizens' groups: to improve the lot of migrant workers; to take action against some form of discrimination; to fight crime; to elect an official; to protect consumers from fraud; to do away with a pesticide that is killing wildlife.

One does not need to be a citizen to join in such activities. Once you settle into a community (even a big city), you will soon be aware of the varieties of voluntary work that are going on around you. Anyone who is interested in sharing this side of American life will greatly deepen his understanding of the country. A place to start is by calling a Volunteer Center or contacting a local church, YMCA or similar organizations. Asking neighbors about what is available often elicits a helpful response.

DO YOU ALREADY BELONG?

Perhaps in your home country you already belong to some group such as Rotary, Lions, YWCA, university women—or to a professional group (journalists, chemical engineers, doctors, and so on). Perhaps you belong to a sports club—ski, tennis, soccer, or hiking—or a university alumni group. (Many overseas universities have alumni chapters scattered around the United States.)

If you are already a member of any such organization at home, look for its affiliate here and let them know of your desire to participate. You will get an immediate welcome. If you are interested in, but not yet affiliated with, any such group, try to become a member before leaving your own country. You will then automatically be eligible to join activities with your American counterparts on arrival without waiting for membership formalities. Such channels for making new friends will be most useful when you first arrive, so it is good to come with introductions and with memberships already established, if you can.

INTEREST GROUPS

There are of course many sports and activities which anyone can do without joining formal organizations. Hunters and fishermen can find colleagues here in great numbers, as can climbers, hikers, or skiers; so can bridge players, photographers, chess enthusiasts, bird watchers, or cello players! Whatever your nationality, you can also find a national group in any large city. Ask at your nearest consulate or look under "Associations" in the Classified Directory to find the Turkish Society, India House, African Center, or whatever exists locally.

Mah-jong or chess players, stamp collectors, those who seek a small informal orchestra, or others with special interests should ask their friends, neighbors, and office colleagues where to find such groups. Every locality has them. Often the local librarian can give you leads or you will find them listed under "Clubs" in the telephone book (Classified). Language problems would hardly bother you at all in any such gathering. Rarely are such clubs exclusive; generally they are eager for new and interested members. Do not feel shy in explaining that you have just arrived from another country and are looking for people who share your interest and enthusiasm.

You will find that expressed interest in taking part in something will open doors for you. Americans like active, energetic people. This is the way we ourselves meet each other as we keep moving to new communities within our own country. Out of such shared interests come invitations into people's homes and gradually into the life of the locality.

HAVE YOU ALWAYS MEANT TO STUDY?

Perhaps for a while when you first come to America you will want to study English—or to join an English conversation group in order to gain confidence in speaking.

Or perhaps you will have time to acquire some new skills, to take a short course that has always interested you or finish one that needs to be completed.

One secretary at the United Nations took a stenotyping course in her free evenings. By the time she returned home to Malaysia she was able to command twice her previous salary by expert reporting of meetings and conferences. Later she opened a small stereotyping school in her own country and again more than doubled her salary!

Adult education is widespread. Classes are offered in every known thing: painting, cooking, photography, languages, astronomy, being a travel agent, programming computers. One need not necessarily have any particular qualifications to enroll in a wide range of classes.

Some people may be interested in taking more substantive and longer courses leading to degrees, certificates, or diplomas of various kinds. Possibilities include: journalism, interior decorating, fashion design, business administration, accounting, and so on.

Both classes and courses are advertised in local newspapers, especially on Sundays and at the change of terms (that is, September, January, or June). Look under "Schools" in the telephone book (Classified). YM, and YWCA's offer a wide range of classes; the public school systems of most cities sponsor adult evening classes. Ask for a catalogue of adult courses from the local Board of Education.

In addition, if you are near any of the nation's 1,800 colleges and universities, you will find they make available courses, concerts and lectures to the nearby community. Usually these are held in the evening. You can ask to be put on their mailing list for advance notices.

LECTURES

Americans love lectures! If you like to be intellectually stimulated but do not have time for a complete course, you can follow any line of interest on a more casual basis—often free. You may want to explore new fields like oceanography, city planning, or outer space!

In addition to lectures given at colleges and universities, you will find that botanical gardens, civil rights organizations, government and political groups, churches, and museums also offer a great number of lectures, debates, and forums; so do international organizations, business groups, and professional bodies.

Get yourself on mailing lists (usually free for the asking), listen to local radio announcements, or ask your friends' advice. Easiest of all—just read the newspapers.

MUSEUMS CAN BE ENGROSSING

If your idea of a museum is a dusty, musty row of glass cases or rooms full of miserably lit oil paintings, try afresh. The art of display itself has become highly developed in this country so that museums have come "alive" in the past years to an extraordinary degree.

In addition to many fine art museums, look also for natural history museums. Photographic exhibits are often a particularly good way to understand the social concerns of a country. Don't miss the many small museums of contemporary crafts, Black history, American Indian history, musical instruments, coins. While at the museum one can often rent a small tape-recorded guide which adds much to one's understanding (rental fees are generally modest for two or three hours use). Sometimes they are available in several languages. Those going to Boston, Austin, Texas, New York, Austin (Texas), Philadelphia, Washington, D.C., Atlanta, Chicago, Denver, or San Francisco should plan to spend considerable time at the particularly fine museums in these cities.

Places like Williamsburg, Virginia; Deerborn, Michigan; and Sturbridge Village, Massachusetts are whole villages, reconstructed as living museums to depict the life of our early settlers. At most times of the year there are live demonstrations of many old crafts such as candle-making, quilting, or the shoeing of horses. There are similar waterfront "museums" at Mystic, Connecticut or the Seaports of New York or Baltimore, where one can board old sailing vessels. Ask for similar historic centers near any locality where you settle.

DO YOU LIKE THEATER? MUSIC? DANCE?

The country abounds in these arts, both professional and amateur. Most large cities have their own symphony orchestras;

there is a wealth of experimental offbeat drama being produced across the country in college theatres, community centers, and small neighborhood theatres, as well as traditional theatre; there are many Film Festivals; movies are popular.

Theater

Ticket prices for legitimate theater in the big cities have soared; so have the prices of movies in major theaters. However, you can avoid these by going to smaller theaters which often have the same performances, but at lower prices. Many cities now subsidize a City Center, keeping prices at a reasonable level. Ask New Yorkers about "twofers"—meaning two tickets for the price of one. Sometimes at the end of a long and successful Broadway run, or when promoters are trying to fill a faltering house for an unknown artist, these become available. Often you can use them to see excellent productions at half price.

Theater, opera, and concert tickets are often hard to come by —partly because the population of cities is mushrooming, partly because public taste is growing more and more arts-minded. There are various ways to obtain tickets—besides the usual one of going to the box office weeks in advance.

Read the theater reviews in local newspapers, then *write in* quickly for tickets, sending a check or money order with your request. This is the best way if you have lots of time, but be *sure* to send a *self-addressed and stamped* envelope or you will get no answer. If you can offer two or three dates, your chance of getting one of them is far better than if you specify only one. Sometimes all the tickets in the house are taken over on a given night for a charity or special "outing." So give alternate dates if you possibly can, and write as far ahead as practical.

If theater is important to you, you can join a "theater club" in most cities and get tickets through them. They usually open their membership in September. Watch the theater section of the newspapers for advertisements. They send members reviews of plays before they open, as well as giving them the chance to buy tickets by mail in advance at reduced rates.

Discount tickets and theatre vouchers are also available through various organizations in many cities. Ask your colleagues and read the "Arts and Leisure" section of your local newspaper. In addition, many cities sponsor free performances of many kinds in parks, schools, libraries, and other centers.

Music

Almost your only hope of getting tickets for opera and major concerts in most cities is to take out a season ticket, by subscription. Look into this long before September 1, if you can. Renewals are offered to old subscribers in June. Then series go on public sale. As these are apt to be expensive, it is quite usual for several people to join together to buy one "series." They then divide the tickets among themselves, each couple going once or twice a month. This is perfectly legitimate and often done.

Another method of securing tickets for a particular performance is through ticket brokers. You pay (legally) a bit more per ticket. These brokers handle about 5 percent of all theater and concert tickets sold in a big city like New York.

You will find brokers in the telephone directory (Classified) under "Theater Brokers" or "Theater Tickets." You will also find them at desks in the lobbies of most good hotels and clustered around the theater district.

Dance

"Modern" dance and the Jazz dance form started in the USA and are vibrant American art forms today. Classical ballet is also popular. Much of America's hopes, fears, ideals, tensions, and culture are clearly visible through its dance. Those coming from abroad can learn a great deal about the country by watching, or by participating in classes which exist everywhere.

WHAT ABOUT SPORTS?

Newcomers to the United States often find lack of exercise and sports one of their hardest adjustments. Actually, it need not be so. Almost all sports are available everywhere, even in a city such as New York with all its mortar, steel, and glass. One of the first places to investigate if you are interested in swimming, tennis, badminton, gym classes, modern dance, or anything of an indoor sport nature is the nearest YM or YWCA. Most of these are well equipped and provide excellent facilities for reasonable fees. There are fancier and more expensive facilities for all such sports as well, often at clubs or hotels.

Swimming

A great many swimming pools are open to the public. In addition to those run by the YW or YMCA, others are operated by the cities or towns themselves or by hotels or swimming schools. When weather permits, there are often public and private beaches available within easy distance. Usually these can be reached by public transport—either bus or train—as well as by private car. Look in the classified pages of the telephone book under "Swimming" or "Sports."

Other Sports

Read the newspapers or look in the telephone book under the name of whatever sport interests you, and you will find: ski trips (day or weekend), walking clubs, fencing, gymnasiums, judo and karate classes, ice skating, squash and racquetball, bicycle clubs, riding groups, bird watchers. One of this country's favorite sports is bowling. In addition to private clubs, nearly all cities maintain numerous tennis courts and golf courses which are open to the public for small fees. Ask your local Department of Parks and Recreation for booklets describing their sports facilities.

Those who like baseball need only drift around the parks. Many games will be going on. Usually they need and welcome additional players. Roller-skating, Frisbee-throwing, kite-flying, and fun with plane or sailboat models are all popular, especially in parks; one can also find paths for biking, jogging, or walking in these areas.

Camping and Hiking

Within relatively easy access (by bus or car) one will find excellent camping facilities in both state and national parks.

One can get free booklets and maps describing camp facilities and park areas by writing both to the individual state and the National Parks Department. It is advisable to get information from both by addressing letters to both:

State: Department of Parks, State Capitol, State (as appropriate for your state);

National: National Parks Department, Department of the Interior, Washington, D.C.

All over the United States, there are thousands of miles of walking trails, all kinds of lodges and huts, and a great many campsites where you can pitch tents and find water, but you need to know where to find them in order to avoid overcrowded highways, and too many people. You need to make reservations months ahead in these public areas; one of the disadvantages of our vast size and population is that we must often "schedule" solitude in public places.

Fishing and Hunting

The state and national booklets described above also include information for the fisherman and hunter. In addition you can always find fellow enthusiasts in your own locality. Talk to your colleagues; read the sports columns in the newspapers; chat with salesmen in the sporting goods stores. Through such contacts, you can find out what clubs there are in the vicinity and then ask about the possibility of joining one. Public-owned facilities are likely to be crowded; joining a group or club gives you access to more private waters and woods. Most clubs have reasonably open membership rules and would welcome your inquiry. They range in price from moderate to high; the lower the price the more welcoming they are in general, but also, of course, the more crowded. The expensive clubs, are, of course, likely to be the most exclusive.

Birds

Those interested in birds should look up the nearest Audubon Society in the telephone book and ask about groups, activities, or sanctuaries that exist in the area. The local library is another good source of information.

Deep-Sea Fishing

Deep-sea fishermen will find boats and salty old captains ready to take them out at almost any marina or port. Prices per day are high, but you can avoid this if you make up a group and go together, thus dividing the cost among many of you.

WATCHING AMERICANS AT WORK

There are many people who do not want to become deeply involved with American activities but who still are interested in learning about the country. They are welcome to "watch the wheels go round" if they so desire. It is easy to watch a nation work when you visit people at their jobs.

If you cannot find out about possibilities through your friends, just call the place of business that most interests you (factory, bank, police training school, or whatever). Ask for the Public Relations Department. They will be able to tell you whether they have tours or whether you can visit on your own. Tell them where you are from and why you are interested. In most cases you will find that people are friendly and pleased to have you visit as their guest, although they first may check with your office to make sure you are bonafide. Do not tip or pay any fee, but a thank-you letter afterward would be much appreciated.

You can visit most kinds of factories and watch men and women working at heavy industry, precision manufacturing, or food-processing. You can call on various kinds of schools; watch courts in progress; listen to hearings before government committees; attend town meetings, or meetings of school boards. Rarely are any of these private. Usually the public is admitted, although sometimes only by previous arrangement. You can often go aboard ocean liners in the big ports. Often there are tours for the public "behind the scenes" in such places as department stores, post offices, or newspaper plants.

The thing to remember in this country is not to be shy or retiring. We welcome guests; we are flattered to have people interested in what we are doing; we are proud to show them what we have. The secret, however, is to make arrangements in advance, be sure your visit will be convenient to the other person, then be *on time*.

This country is yours—full of variety, full of welcome. It is so big and moves at so swift a pace that it can pass you by if you do not stretch out your hands to it. But anyone who wants to join in and is not too shy to make himself or herself known to the people around will find a ready welcome. You will have more to do than time to do it in once you begin!

We are glad you are coming; we hope your experiences here will be rich and happy.

Appendix

Appendix

Part I

Dull but Important Formalities

VISAS

If you are not planning to settle permanently in the United States, you are likely to be classified as a "non-immigrant" alien. This means that to enter the country you will need a visa as well as a passport and health record.

There are various kinds of visas depending on the estimated length of stay and, even more important, the purpose and auspices of the visit. (Canadians, British residents of Canada, and Mexicans who have Border Crossing cards do not need visas.)

To get a visa, you present your passport to the nearest U.S. Consulate.

Among types of visas available are:

B 1, B 2

Normal short visits for business = B 1
Normal short visits for pleasure = B 2

With either of these, you may not work for pay.

F 1, F 2

Student = F 1
Family of student = F 2

J 1, J 2

Exchange visitor on a State Department program = J 1
Spouse or children of exchange visitor = J 2

H 1

For aliens coming temporarily who are of distinguished merit and ability, usually entertainers, sports stars, lecturers, etc., offering services of an exceptional nature.

H 2

Aliens coming for short-term special work with skills not readily available in the United States.

H 3

Industrial trainees coming to the U.S. for training in work they will return to do abroad on completion of program.

A small white form, 1-94, will be stapled into your passport which will show the classification under which you arrived, the arrival date, the purpose of the visit, and (most important) the departure date assigned to you by the U.S. Immigration and Naturalization Service. If you want to stay longer than the date on this form, you must apply for an "Extension of Stay" *at least one month* before the expiration date. Ask at the nearest Immigration and Naturalization Service office for the necessary form to fill out.

Don't let your visa expire by mistake! You would be surprised how many people do. If you overstay your date without an approved extension, you will find yourself going through enormous amounts of red tape.

ALIEN REGISTRATION

If you are over twenty-one years old and in the United States past the turn of any calendar year (January 1st), you must fill out a short alien registration card (1-53) during the month of January. This applies to each member of a family over twenty-one. The purpose of this form is merely to give the Department of Justice a yearly check on the addresses of aliens. Forms can be obtained at any post office. There is no charge. Just ask for them at the counter during the month of January. If you fail to do this, you could be deported.

TAXES

Those working for a corporation will be advised about taxes by their firm; others should consult a tax expert in their bank or a lawyer. Avoid the "tax advisors" who advertise in the streets; many of these are not reliable. Go to someone you can trust.

In the United States most people pay at least two forms of Income Tax: Federal and State. In some areas they also pay a City Tax. Even if you live in one state, you may pay the tax of another if you earn your money there. For example, people who live in New Jersey or Connecticut pay a New York City tax on what they earn in that city. They also pay a New York state tax.

A booklet, *U.S. Guide for Aliens,* has been published and is available free of charge if ordered directly from the Internal Revenue Service Office in the area where you settle. Or you can write for it to the Superintendent of Documents, U.S. Government Printing Office, Washington, D.C. 20402

Anyone who has been in the country for 90 days in one year or who has earned over $3,000 in one year should check to see if he is liable for payment of taxes. He should also find out whether or not he is covered by a treaty between the United States and his home country. Some countries have such treaties which grant certain exemptions from U.S. taxes. The normal rule is that a person is liable for taxation by only one country, his own or the United States, but not both. Not all countries have such agreements, however. Be sure to know about your own. You can get this information from your own or the U.S. embassy or consulate. Even when such agreements do exist, the details vary. Some countries will refund some of the taxes paid in the United States, but you may have to pay first and argue later!

Filing Dates

If you are being taxed as a "non-resident alien" and you have no wages subject to withholding, you file you income tax return *on or before June 15.*

If your status is "resident alien" for income tax purposes, or if you are a "non-resident alien" but you are receiving wages that are subject to withholding, you must file *on or before April 15.*

Even if you do not have to actually pay any tax, you will almost surely need to file a return. Ask, ask, ask! It is better to be sure than sorry.

As in all bureaucracies, you may get a bit of a run-around or be kept waiting or have to fill out a great many forms. Bear with it; in the long run these people are trying to help you with your tax questions before problems or penalties arise.

Before Leaving the United States

Before returning home, you will have to satisfy the U.S. Internal Revenue Service that your taxes have been paid. To obtain a Sailing (or exit) Permit you will need to fill out Form 1040C or Form 2063.

You will be asked to submit this form together with:

1) Your passport;
2) Alien registration card (if you have one);
3) Copy of any previous year's returns and proof of tax paid (if you have this);
4) Statement from your employer as to wages earned and taxes already paid;
5) Report of any other income in the current year on which there is no withholding (if you made speeches, or wrote articles, for example);
6) Any other records and documents such as receipts, bank records, canceled checks, etc., that substantiate business expenses.

WHAT YOU CAN BRING THROUGH CUSTOMS

You may be asking yourself, "What can I bring into the United States without paying duty?" "Can I bring gifts?" "Must I declare *everything?*" "Is there anything that I may not bring?"

You should obtain a copy of a pamphlet, *Customs Hints for Visi-*

tors (Nonresidents), giving full answers to all such questions from the nearest U.S. Consulate.

Not Allowed

Some things may *not* be brought into the United States without special permits:

1) *Drugs*

If you must bring in a special prescription, be *sure* to get a permit in advance. Inquire at the U.S. Consulate for details.

2) *Plants*

No fruits, vegetables, plants, seeds, cuttings, or plant products may be imported without writing *ahead* for permission from:

Import and Permit Section
Plant Quarantine Division
209 River Street
Hoboken, New Jersey 07030

The reason for this regulation is that the country is attempting to prevent insects or plant diseases from being brought in by mistake.

3) *Meats and Hides*

To avoid animal diseases, permission is needed to bring in meats (including sausages, salamis, etc.); untanned furs or hides; cattle, horses, burros, etc; wildfowl or barnyard fowl (including eggs for hatching!).

If you wish to bring them in, write to:

Animal Health Division
U.S. Agricultural Research Service
Hyattsville, Maryland 20782

4) *Goods from Certain Countries*

One cannot import goods of any kind originating in Cambodia, Cuba, North Korea, Vietnam.

Inquiries should be made to:

Foreign Assets Control
Department of the Treasury
Washington, D.C. 20220

5) *Gold*

There are tight restrictions regarding gold, gold coins, gold coin jewelry or medals.

6) *Firearms and Ammunition*

Guns and ammunition for sporting purposes only, may be imported with permission from:

Firearms Division
Internal Revenue Service
Washington, D.C. 20224

No ammunition, pistols, or revolvers may be shipped in the U.S. mails.

Pets

Cats, dogs, monkeys, etc., must meet certain requirements before they may enter. Ask at the nearest U.S. Consulate for the booklet *So You Want to Import a Pet* or write:

Foreign Quarantine Program
U.S. Public Health Service
National Communicable Disease Center
Atlanta, Georgia 30333

Questions

If you have questions on Customs regulations that cannot be answered by your nearest U.S. Embassy or Consulate, write:

Bureau of Customs
Department of the Treasury
Washington, D.C. 20226

Part II

Household Helps

CENTIGRADE AND FAHRENHEIT

To change Centigrade into Fahrenheit multiply by 9/5 and then add 32.

You may find it easier to learn a few of the most common temperature measures by heart!

CENTIGRADE		FAHRENHEIT
−18°		0°
0°		32°
10°		50°
20°	(room temp.)	68°
30°		86°
40°		104°
100°	(boiling)	212°

Body temperature: 26.9 °C is 98.6 °F.

METRICS AND AMERICAN MEASURES

This country is one of the last not to be using the metric system! We are starting to change over but you may need some help in adjusting to our system of measures:

mile   a little over two kilometers; multiply kilometers by .6 to get miles

pound   approximately one-half kilogram; a kilogram is actually 2.2 pounds

yard   just short of a meter which is 11/10 of a yard. One U.S. *foot,* which is 12 *inches,* is 30.4 centimeters. One meter is 3.2 feet (a yard is 3 feet).

inch   about three centimeters (a centimeter is 3/10 of an inch). 91
            centimeters is one U.S. yard.

quart   almost the size of a liter (the liter is 11/10 of a quart). Gasoline
            is sold by the *gallon,* which is four quarts.

ounce   approximately 30 grams. There are 16 ounces in a pound. For
            measures smaller than an ounce, Americans divide the ounce:
            ½ ounce, ½ ounce, etc.

CLOTHING SIZES

Throughout the world, countries are attempting to standardize sizes. However, there is still so much variation that shopping is always difficult when one first moves to another land.

Even with a size-conversion chart, you would do well to shop with your tape measure in hand and, above all, try clothing on. Shapes, fullness, armholes, proportion of body size to neckband or sleeve length vary according to national origin. If your size is not "standard" by American measures, you may have to search a bit among unfamiliar terms such as "Junior Miss" or "Petite," "King Size" or "Stout Size" or "Out Size." Large department stores often have what they call "Personal Shopping Departments" or "Service Desks" where you can get help if you ask for it. Many major stores in large cities have salespeople who can speak a number of languages.

The following comparison of American with European sizes may be helpful to Asians, Africans, or South Americans as well, since many countries follow either British or Continental measures. Please realize, however, that there is much variation from country to country and even within countries as well. The information below, therefore, is included only as a guide and is not to be taken as necessarily an exact measure.

WOMEN

Dresses and Coats—Misses

U.S.A.	8	10	12	14	16	18	20
British	—	10	12	14	16	18	20
Continental	—	38	40	42	44	46	48

Dresses and Coats—Women's

U.S.A.	34	36	38	40	44	44
British	34	36	38	40	42	44
Continental	42	44	46	48	50	52

Dresses and Coats—Junior

U.S.A. and						
British	7	9	11	13	15	17
Continental	34	35	38	40	42	44

Stockings

U.S.A. and						
British	8	8½	9	10	10½	11
Continental	0	1	2	4	5	6

(But many European countries use the same as the U.S.A.)

Blouses, Sweaters, Slips

U.S.A. and						
British	30	32	34	36	38	40
Continental	38	40	42	44	46	48

Shoes

U.S.A.	5	5½	6	7	8	8½	9
British	3½	4	4½	5½	6½	7	7½
Continental	35	35	36	38	38½	39	40

MEN

Coats and Suits

U.S.A.	36	38	40	42	44	46
European	46	48	50	54	56	59

Shirts

U.S.A.	14½	15	15½	16	16½
European	37	38	39	40	41

Shoes and Slippers

U.S.A.	8	8½	9½	10	10½
European	41	42	43	44	45

Americans often use the sizes Small, Medium, Large, or Extra Large.

FOR WOMEN:

Small	Sizes under 12;
Medium	Sizes 14-16 and sometimes also 12;
Large	18 and up; sometimes also 16.

In skirts, dresses, coats, half sizes are usually intended for the short-waisted, stocky figure.

FOR MEN:

Small   Sizes under 36 British or American or 46 European;
Medium 36-38 British or 46-48 Europeon;
Large   *40 British, 40 European; anything over is Extra Large.*

TRANSLATING COOKING MEASURES

Since recipes and measures will often be given in what will at first
be unfamiliar terms, be *sure* to bring your own measuring spoons
and cups. Americans rarely use scales in home cooking. The following measures may be helpful.

In General:

Since a liter is about a *quart,* a half liter is a *pint.*

A pound is 500 grams, so think of ½ pound as 250 grams;
densities make a difference, however, so a cup of sugar is 200 grams,
whereas a cup of flour is only 150!

AMERICAN SPOONS	LIQUID GRAMS	FRENCH MEASURES
1 teaspoon (t., or tsp.)	2	1 cuillere a cafe
1 tablespoon (T., or tbsp.)	6	1 cuillere a soupe cuillere a bouche or: verre a liquer
6⅔ teaspoon	100	1 deilitre 1 demi-verre
16 tablespoon = 1 cup (c.)	22	¼ litre (less 2 tbsp.)

AMERICAN CUPS	LIQUID GRAMS	FRENCH MEASURES
1 cup = ½ pint (pt.)	22	½ litre (less 2 tbsp.)
2 cups = 1 pint or ½ pound (lb.)	454	½ litre less ½ decilitre
4 cups =1 quart (qt.)	907	%₁₀ of a litre
4 quarts = 1 gallon (gal.)		3.8 litres

or, to put it differently:

> 1 litre = 4⅓ cups (U.S.A.)
> ¼ litre = 1 cup plus 1 tbsp.
> 1 decilitre = 6⅔ tbsp.
> 250 grams = ½ pound (U.S.A.)

OVEN SETTINGS MAY BE CONFUSING

AMERICAN OVENS DEGREES		CENTIGRADE	FRENCH	BRITISH
140°-250°	Low or "Slow"	70°-121°	"Douce" (#1, #2, #3)	#¼-#1
300°-400°	Moderate	150°-205°	"Moyen" (#5)	#2-#5
400° up	High or "Hot"	205° up	"Vif" (#6 up)	#6 up

CUTS OF MEAT ARE DIFFERENT

There are basic differences in the way meat is cut in different parts of the world. Primarily these differences fall into two methods:

1) The meat is *muscle boned;* the different muscles are separated;
2) The meat is *unboned;* the retail cuts are sliced across the muscles, bones, and fat.

In the United States, meat is *unboned.* As a result, many cuts have more than one muscle in them, and the degree of tenderness may vary. However, most of the natural fat is left on the meat and because the meat is held on the bones while it is being cooked, there is less shrinkage and added flavor. So there are pluses and minuses to both methods.

One notices the difference most clearly in beef because the animal is so large. Veal, lamb, and pork are butchered in about the same way.

GRADES AND QUALITIES OF FOODS

The government is trying to make it easier for shoppers to tell the quality of food before buying it. Grading is carried on by the U.S.

Department of Agriculture (abbreviated as USDA). Since it is not required by law that all producers use this service, all foods do not necessarily carry the seal even when the quality is of top level. However, if you learn to recognize and look for the shields, they can help you to know what you are buying. Foods most likely to carry them are beef, veal, poultry, eggs and butter. *(Note:* The best grade is listed first.)

Beef, Veal, Lamb: U.S. Prime, Choice, Good, Standard

Poultry: U.S. Grades A and B

Watch for the words "Young" or "Broiler" or "Fryer." These all mean the bird is tender. "Mature" means you must cook it in moist heat to tenderize it, or it is likely to be tough.

Eggs: U.S. Grade AA, A, B

Eggs are also classified by size: Extra Large, Large, Medium, and Small. It you see the word "Jumbo," it means biggest of all!

Butter: U.S. Grades AA, A, and B

Grade A is almost as good as AA—the average person cannot tell any difference— and is far cheaper.

Canned, frozen, dried Fruits and Vegetables: 1) U.S. Grade A or U.S. Fancy, 2) U.S. Grade B or U.S. Choice, or sometimes Extra Standard, 3) U.S. Grade C or U.S. Standard

Apples: These come under a number of gradations: U.S. Extra Fancy, U.S. Fancy, U.S. No. 1 (note that this is actually the *third* level), U.S. Utility (Good for applesauce, but not for eating uncooked).